THE

BOOZY

BAKER

THE
BOOZY
BAKER

75

RECIPES FOR
SPIRITED
SWEETS

by **LUCY BAKER**

Running Press
PHILADELPHIA · LONDON

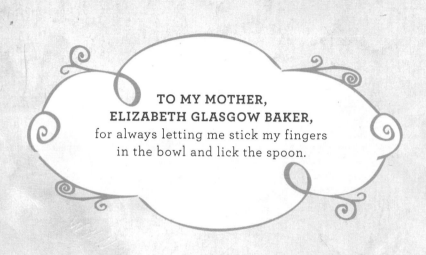

**TO MY MOTHER,
ELIZABETH GLASGOW BAKER,**
for always letting me stick my fingers
in the bowl and lick the spoon.

9 8 7 6 5 4 3 2 1
Digit on the right indicates the number of this printing

Library of Congress Control Number: 2009940779

ISBN 978-0-7624-3802-0

Edited by Geoffrey Stone
Cover and interior design by Amanda Richmond
Typography: Archer, Geetype, Verlag and Chronicle

Food styling by Katrina Tekavec
Special thanks to Mariellen Melker, Manor Home & Gifts, Philadelphia, PA;
Scarlett Alley, Philadelphia, PA; Fosters Urban Housewares, Philadelphia, PA;
Home Grown, Haverford, PA; Crate & Barrel, King of Prussia, PA;
and Kitchen Kapers, King of Prussia, PA for the props.

Running Press Book Publishers
2300 Chestnut Street
Philadelphia, PA 19103-4371

Visit us on the web!
www.runningpresscooks.com

CONTENTS

ACKNOWLEDGMENTS

Enormous thanks to my agent, Sharon Bowers, for encouraging me to write my own book and stick to the deadlines. Also to Jennifer Griffin and Angela Miller for their unparalleled input and support. Thanks to my editor, Geoffrey Stone, for believing that baking with booze was an excellent idea, and for shaping my vision into printed reality. Thanks to Amanda Richmond for her inspired design, Katrina Tekavec for her lovely styling, and to Steve Legato for the gorgeous photographs.

I'm especially grateful to Ed Levine and the entire team at SeriousEats.com for entrusting me with a weekly column, teaching me to blog, and sharing my obsession with food. A big thank you to Natalie Danford for setting a terrific example of a working food writer. Thank you to Tom Birchard and Lisa Staub, Bruce Weinstein and Mark Scarbrough, and Rick Rodgers for allowing me to add a little sauce to their recipes and include them here.

Thank you to all of my wonderful friends, especially Bryan Rucker and Peter Chapin for the cocktail suggestions; Sarah Izzo, Mary Cavett, Sarah Kramer, and Robbie Fenster for the recipe testing and tasting; and Blythe Miller for relinquishing the kitchen.

I am forever in gratitude to my parents, John and Elizabeth Baker, and my brother, Jeffrey, for cheering me on unconditionally, and for occasionally letting me hold the rotating title of "Best in the Fam."

Most of all, thank you to Alex Brandes, for loving me and supporting my dreams, and always honestly answering the question, "But is it bakery good?"

Last but not least, thank you to the amazing Harriet Bell, my friend, mentor, and first-ever boss, for teaching me everything I know about cookbooks, and to never use the phrase "mouthwatering."

iNTRODUCTiON

*"So take up your bottle opener and your jigger, dear explorer,
and go—where're your daring and the spirit moves you!"*

—RUTH VENDLEY NEUMANN, COOKING WITH SPIRITS, 1961

Here is a memory: I am six years old, standing in the kitchen in a nightgown covered with tiny purple flowers. I have just finished breakfast. My mother is on the phone in the other room. With silent, barefoot steps, I approach the counter and place my palms facedown on its top. Then I take a deep breath, muster all my strength, and hoist my chubby little body onto the surface.

I freeze and cock my head to the side, listening to make sure that my mom hasn't heard me.

When I'm confident that she's still engrossed in conversation, I continue with my mission. Bit by bit I inch my way across the countertop: past the sink filled with soaking cereal bowls, past the toaster, past the breadbox overflowing with English muffins, and even past the open package of Entenmann's miniature powdered donuts. Today, I will not be distracted.

Finally, I stop in front of a cabinet that I have watched my mom rummage through countless times. I ease open the cabinet door, wincing as it creaks a little. Then I lean in and inhale the heady, spicy smells emanating from all the tiny jars and containers.

There, perched way up on the top shelf is what I have been looking for: the brown glass bottle of vanilla extract.

Whenever my mom baked a batch of her famous fudgy brownies, or the raisin cupcakes from a recipe passed down from my grandmother, she added a teaspoonful of vanilla. It was my favorite part of the baking process. Vanilla extract was the most wonderful-smelling thing in the world: warm and sweet, like a mixture of flowers and ice cream. Surely, I thought, it must taste even better.

I snatched down the bottle and unscrewed the red plastic cap. Then I tilted it to my lips and took a giant swig, pouring about a quarter of the contents into my mouth. It tasted terrible. Like medicine. Gasping and sputtering, I spit the vanilla out in a shower of brown drops that splattered down the front of my nightgown. I coughed loudly and lost my balance, tumbling from the counter to the floor, landing startled but safely on my bottom.

My mom came running. "What happened?"

"I wanted to try the vanilla. I thought it would taste like it smells."

"Oh, Honey!" Laughing, she explained that vanilla extract didn't contain any sugar. It was made mostly of alcohol.

Strange. I remember thinking, why would anyone want to bake cakes or cookies with that?

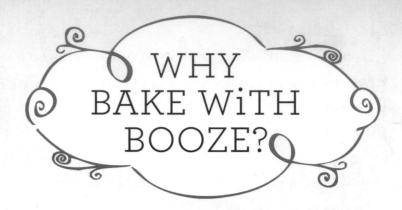

WHY BAKE WiTH BOOZE?

Years later, after I had grown up (sort of) and become a food writer, I discovered the answer to my childhood question: we bake with booze because alcohol—from spirits, such as bourbon and rum, to liqueurs like amaretto and crème de menthe, to wine and beer—imparts a subtle, sumptuous warmth that deepens the flavors of desserts and makes them taste even more decadent, luxurious, and sinful. A pear crisp straight from the oven is much more comforting with a generous dose of merlot, and whoopie pies take on a grown-up twist when filled with Grand Marnier-infused marshmallow cream.

Besides, baking with booze is fun—plain and simple. Infusing desserts with different alcohols is an easy way for "weekend foodies" (people who may not have gone to culinary school but who read cookbooks like novels and Tivo the Food Network) to add a "saucy" twist to what they bake—no kugelhopf pan or flute-tipped pastry bag required.

Lots of us turn to food and drink for comfort: after an argument with a friend, in the middle of a tough workweek, or on a cold and rainy day. Sometimes, in these difficult moments, a cupcake crowned with a cloud of frosting or an unusual take on a classic cocktail is all we need to brighten our spirits. People have always looked for consolation in the bottle—and in the cookie jar. Why not combine the two in one?

What's that you say? You don't exactly have a fully stocked bar? Not to worry. Most of the sumptuous, saucy recipes in these pages come with easy substitutions for swapping port and framboise, rum and tequila, brandy and bourbon, so you don't have to buy a whole bottle just to bake one dessert. Moreover, you just might find a way to use up that bottle of coconut rum that has been gathering dust since your last Tiki party. (When was your last Tiki party?)

Whether you are a pastry-perfectionist or a one-bowl beginner, a bona fide mixologist or a cocktail neophyte, it's time to get out your shaker and your oven mitts. I hope this book becomes a favorite, its pages splattered with chocolate, sprinkled with sugar . . . and garnished with a twist.

Homemade Bourbon Vanilla Extract

3 vanilla beans
1 cup bourbon

Rinse a clean, empty jam jar or a mason jar with boiling water to sterilize it. Set aside. Split the vanilla beans in half lengthwise with a small, sharp knife. Add them to the jar. Pour the bourbon over the vanilla beans and screw the jar's lid on tightly. Give the jar a few good shakes. Place the jar in a cool, dark cabinet or closet and let it steep for 8 weeks, shaking occasionally. The extract will darken over time. Homemade Bourbon Vanilla Extract can be used in place of store-bought vanilla extract in any recipe. There is no need to remove the vanilla beans.

MAKES
1 CUP

iNGREDiENTS

We've all heard the adage "baking is a science." It's true in many respects. If cake flour is wantonly substituted for all-purpose flour, or if two eggs are used instead of the requisite four because that's all that's left in the fridge, the recipe will fail.

But baking isn't quite an exact science. If dry ingredients are whisked instead of sifted, if a dash of salt is omitted, or if a pinch of cinnamon is accidentally doubled, try not to worry about it. This isn't high school chemistry class, with the dorky rubber goggles and the drippy lab partner. There are no grades (only dessert), and no one is going to complain as long as the recipes are baked with love, top-notch ingredients—and plenty of booze.

BUTTER: Good butter lies at the soul of every great baking recipe, and there is no substitute for the real thing. All of my recipes call for unsalted butter, which tends to taste a bit fresher than salted versions. Also, the amount of salt in salted butter varies from brand to brand. Using unsalted butter allows the baker to control the level of salt in a recipe. If circumstances are dire and salted butter must be used, simply omit the salt from the rest of the recipe.

MILK AND CREAM: I use whole milk in all my recipes. Low-fat milk can be substituted, but not skim milk, which is far too watery. If low-fat milk is used, the dessert will not be as rich or creamy in texture. The one exception to this rule is buttermilk, which is more readily available in reduced-fat versions, and is naturally quite thick. I use heavy cream (sometimes labeled "whipping cream") in these recipes. For the best flavor, use the freshest cream available. For some recipes, such as the Banana-Rum-Raisin Rice Pudding or the Donut Bread Pudding with Tennessee Whiskey Sauce, half-and-half can be substituted for the cream. When preparing whipped cream to garnish a dessert, never substitute light cream or half-and-half.

EGGS: I use large eggs in all these recipes. Buy the freshest available.

FLOUR: I used national-brand, all-purpose flour, such as Gold Medal, when testing these recipes. Use any all-purpose flour or unbleached all-purpose flour. For the recipes that call for cake flour, use any national brand, such as Swans Down.

SUGAR: When a recipe calls for "sugar," stick with white granulated cane sugar. Light and dark brown sugars should be packed into the measuring cup or measuring spoon to ensure accuracy. In a pinch, substitute light brown sugar for dark and vice versa. Do not make any substitutions for confectioners' sugar. For the cocktail recipes, I use superfine sugar, which dissolves faster than regular granulated sugar, or simple syrup. To make simple syrup, combine equal parts water and granulated sugar in a saucepan and simmer until the sugar dissolves.

COCOA POWDER: I use natural unsweetened cocoa powder, as opposed to Dutch-processed, in these recipes. Any quality supermarket brand will do, such as Ghirardelli or Hershey's.

CHOCOLATE: Most of my recipes call for either bittersweet or semisweet chocolate. Use whichever you prefer (bittersweet is darker and semisweet has more sugar). When purchasing chocolate at the supermarket, I often reach for Ghirardelli, Hershey's, or Baker's (for unsweetened chocolate). Premium blends, such as Lindt and Valrhona, are excellent but expensive. If I know I'm going to be doing a lot of baking, I often prefer to buy in bulk. Stores like Trader Joe's sell giant, one-pound chocolate bars at a discount.

When selecting white chocolate, make sure that it contains cocoa butter.

When a recipe calls for melted chocolate, such as the Raspberry Swirl Brownies or the Mocha Cookie Tart, always use chopped chocolate. Do not substitute chocolate chips, which contain stabilizers and won't melt as smoothly.

NUTS: Many of these recipes call for a cup or more of nuts. Since nuts are costly ingredients I prefer to buy them in bulk at specialty stores. They can go bad quickly—especially pecans and pistachios—so store leftovers in the freezer. To toast nuts, spread them in a single layer on an ungreased baking sheet. Toast in a 350°F oven for six to ten minutes.

VANILLA EXTRACT: Always use pure vanilla extract. I know it costs a lot more than imitation varieties, but take a deep breath and just do it. Trust me. Look for brands labeled "Madagascar" or "Tahitian." Some of these recipes call for vanilla beans, split and seeds scraped. The seeds add incredible flavor to ice creams and puddings—and the tiny black flecks are really pretty, too! If vanilla beans aren't available, substitute a half a teaspoon of extract.

Simple Syrup

**MAKES
1 CUP**

½ cup water
½ cup granulated sugar

Combine the water and sugar in a saucepan over medium-high heat.
Bring to a boil and lower the heat to medium low.
Simmer until the sugar dissolves entirely, 5 to 10 minutes.

THE ALCOHOL ALPHABET

AMARETTO: Sweet, high-alcohol liqueur flavored with almonds.

APRICOT BRANDY: Traditionally a brandy distilled from apricots. Many commercial brands are now made from brandy with added "apricot flavor."

APPLEJACK: Originally a very strong alcohol made from concentrated fermented apples, but now the term more commonly refers to apple-flavored brandy.

ARMAGNAC: A premium brandy from the Armagnac region in southwest France.

BEER: An alcoholic beverage brewed from malted barley and flavored with hops. Available in a range of styles from light (pilsners, ales) to dark (porters, stouts).

BITTERS: Not technically alcoholic, bitters are a highly concentrated mixture of aromatic plants and herbs used to flavor many cocktails.

BOURBON: Whiskey distilled from at least 51 percent corn and aged in oak barrels.

BRANDY: Liquor made from distilled wine or fermented fruit.

CALVADOS: High-quality apple brandy from Normandy, France.

CAMPARI: Bitter Italian aperitif, bright red in color, made from a secret blend of herbs and plants.

CHAMPAGNE: Sparkling wine produced in the Champagne region of France. Less expensive substitutions are Spanish Cava or Italian Prosecco.

CIDER: Beverage made from fermented apple juice. Usually relatively low in alcohol (about 3 percent ABV).

COFFEE LIQUEUR: Sweet, high-alcohol liqueur flavored with coffee.

COGNAC: Premium brandy from the Cognac region of France.

COINTREAU: Premium, colorless liqueur flavored with orange. Less expensive varieties are labeled as Triple Sec.

CRÈME DE BANANE: Highly sweetened liqueur flavored with banana.

CRÈME DE CACAO: Dark or light sweet liqueur with chocolate flavors.

CRÈME DE CASSIS: Ruby-colored liqueur flavored with black currant.

CRÈME DE MENTHE: Peppermint-flavored liqueur available in both clear and green varieties.

DOMAINE DE CANTON: French liqueur made from ginger-infused cognac.

FRAMBOISE: Brandy or liqueur made from raspberries.

FRANGELICO: Sweet, high-alcohol liqueur flavored with hazelnuts.

GIN: Liquor usually made primarily from corn and flavored with juniper berries.

GRAND MARNIER: French liqueur made from cognac and flavored with orange.

IRISH CREAM LIQUEUR: Thick, rich liqueur made from Irish whiskey, cream, and sugar.

JÄGERMEISTER: German liqueur with strong herbal and licorice flavors.

KIRSCH: Clear, cherry-flavored brandy.

LIMONCELLO: Sweet, bright yellow lemon liqueur from Southern Italy.

NOCELLO: Sweet, high-alcohol liqueur flavored with walnuts.

OUZO: Sweet anise-flavored aperitifs from Greece.

PISCO: Peruvian or Chilean liquor made from grapes. "Regular" pisco is clear and mild in flavor, "reserve" pisco is darker in color and has a woody, slightly smoky flavor.

POMEGRANATE LIQUEUR: The most widely available brand of pomegranate liqueur is Palma, which is a sweet and tart blend of pomegranate juice, vodka, and a splash of tequila.

RUM: Liquor distilled from fermented sugarcane available in white and dark varieties. White rum has a light taste and is available in flavored varieties, such as coconut. Dark rum has a deeper, caramel flavor and is often aged. The majority of rums are produced around the Caribbean.

RYE: Liquor made from at least 51 percent rye grain and aged in oak.

SAKE: Japanese rice wine.

SAUTERNES: French dessert wine made from semillon, muscadelle, and sauvingnon blanc grapes that have been infected with "noble rot," a beneficial mold that causes grapes to shrivel and retain intense flavor.

SCHNAPPS: Clear, sweetened, and highly alcoholic, flavored with spices or fruits.

SCOTCH WHISKEY: Scottish whisky made from grain and malt, and divided into two major categories: single and blend. Single malt scotch is a product of one distillery; blended scotch is made from whisky from multiple distilleries.

SOUTHERN COMFORT: Sweet whiskey from the American South flavored with fruit and spices.

TEQUILA: Mexican liquor distilled from the mezcal plant. Gold tequila is aged in oak for at least two years.

VODKA: High-proof alcohol, colorless and with little taste, distilled from fermented grains such as rye or wheat.

WHISKEY: General term for alcohol distilled from fermented grains. At least 80 proof, most whiskeys are aged in oak.

WINE: Alcoholic beverage made from fermented grape juice. Sweet wines, such as port, are fortified with brandy.

HAVE YOUR CAKE AND DRiNK iT TOO

There was a bakery in Massachusetts, where I grew up, that made the most delicious yellow butter cake I have ever tasted. It was a single square layer frosted with white buttercream and decorated at the corners with blue flowers. Scrawled across it were the words "Best Wishes." The cake was supposed to be served at a graduation or a communion. I'm not exactly sure how or why my father started buying it for everyday weeknight desserts, but it quickly became a family staple.

"What's for dinner?" my brother and I would ask, dumping our backpacks by the front door.

"Spaghetti and Best Wishes Cake," my mother would reply.

Eating an "occasion" cake on a random Tuesday night may seem a little strange, but it taught me two important lessons. First, when it comes to dessert, there are no rules. Craving a pumpkin layer cake in the middle of July? Go for it. Randomly feeling festive? Bake a Champagne chiffon cake. There is no reason not to indulge a whim.

Second, the best desserts have a sense of humor and, often, a story behind them. It doesn't matter if the layers are a bit lopsided, or if your cheesecake comes out with a crack or two. As long as you serve big pieces and say brightly, "I made it myself," everyone will love it.

Of course, it also never hurts to announce, "There's booze in it, too!" Which is why I've saturated these recipes with everything from brandy and beer to sake and cinnamon schnapps. As an added bonus, the alcohol actually improves the flavors with time. Many of these cakes (especially the loaves and single layers) taste even more delicious the day after they are baked, making them perfect do-ahead desserts.

Here are a few tips for cake baking success. Make sure your ingredients—especially the butter—are at room temperature before you begin preparing a recipe. Chilly eggs, milk, and butter can lead to a lumpy cake. To soften butter in a hurry, dice it into small chunks and leave it on the counter for 15 minutes. When creaming butter and sugar, beat the mixture for a full 2 to 3 minutes. It may look well combined after only a few seconds, but your cake will be lighter and fluffier if you take the extra time. Invest in a box of plain wooden toothpicks and keep them close to your oven. (I stash mine next to my potholders and oven mitts.) There is no better tool for testing if a cake is done. Lastly, be patient while your cake is cooling. Never try to immediately remove it from the pan as it will likely crumble and tear,

Fig and Orange Cake with Ouzo Glaze

MAKES 8 TO 10 SERVINGS

WHO BRINGS OUZO TO A CASUAL HOUSE PARTY *instead of wine or a six-pack of beer? I have no idea which of my friends gave me a bottle of this potent licorice-flavored Greek liquor, but I owe them many thanks. Unsure of what to do with the leftovers, I came up with this recipe, which is the first cake I ever baked with booze.*

If the figs seem dry, plump them in a bit of ouzo before adding them to the cake. Then use the drained ouzo to make a cocktail with tonic water and a squeeze of fresh orange juice.

FOR THE CAKE:

1 cup all-purpose flour

¾ cup cake flour

2 teaspoons baking powder

½ teaspoon ground cinnamon

¼ teaspoon salt

½ pound (2 sticks) unsalted butter, softened

1 cup sugar

4 large eggs

1 teaspoon pure vanilla extract

2 teaspoons ouzo

Freshly grated zest of one large orange

1 cup chopped dried figs

FOR THE GLAZE:

1 cup confectioners' sugar

2 tablespoons ouzo

Preheat the oven to 350°F. Grease a 9 x 5-inch loaf pan with butter or nonstick spray. Line the bottom with parchment paper and grease the paper. Dust the pan with flour and tap out the excess.

TO MAKE THE CAKE, whisk together the all-purpose flour, cake flour, baking powder, cinnamon, and salt in a medium bowl.

In a large bowl, beat the butter with an electric mixer until creamy, about 2 minutes. Add half of the sugar and beat to combine. Add the rest of the sugar and beat until light and fluffy, about 2 minutes. Add the eggs, one at a time, beating to incorporate after each addition and scraping down the sides of the bowl as necessary. Beat in the vanilla extract, ouzo, and the orange zest.

Add the flour mixture to the butter mixture and beat at low speed just until blended. Fold the figs into the batter with a wooden spoon.

Pour the batter into the prepared pan and bake for 50 to 55 minutes, or until the top is golden and a toothpick inserted into the center comes out clean. Cool the cake in the pan for 15 minutes.

TO MAKE THE GLAZE, combine the confectioners' sugar with the ouzo in a medium bowl and whisk until smooth.

Remove the cake from the pan and place it on a wire rack set over a large plate or a baking sheet. Spoon the ouzo glaze over the cake and allow it to cool completely before serving.

SHAKE IT UP: Substitute Pernod, arrack (an anise-flavored liquor from the Middle East), or absinthe for the ouzo.

Green Tea and Banana Cake
with Sake Syrup

MAKES 8 TO 12 SERVINGS

A LOT OF THE TRENDY SUSHI RESTAURANTS *in my neighborhood serve fancy fusion rolls with ingredients like mango and papaya. The delicate flavors commonly associated with Japanese cuisine (and Japanese wine) pair especially well with tropical fruits. Here, I've given a traditional banana loaf cake an Eastern twist with fragrant green tea powder and a floral sake glaze.*

FOR THE CAKE:

- 2 cups all-purpose flour
- ¾ teaspoon baking powder
- ¼ teaspoon salt
- ¼ pound (1 stick) unsalted butter, softened
- 1 cup granulated sugar
- 3 large eggs
- ½ cup sour cream
- 1 cup mashed ripe banana (about 2 bananas)
- 1 tablespoon green tea powder (matcha)

FOR THE GLAZE:

- ¾ cup confectioners' sugar
- 3 tablespoons sake

Preheat the oven to 350°F. Grease a 9 x 5-inch loaf pan with butter, or spray it with nonstick spray. Line the bottom with parchment paper and butter or spray the paper. Dust the pan with flour and tap out the excess.

TO MAKE THE CAKE, in a medium bowl, whisk together the flour, baking powder, and salt. In a large bowl, beat together the butter and sugar with an electric mixer until light and fluffy, about 2 minutes. Beat in the eggs one at a time, and then beat in the sour cream and the banana. Gradually add the flour mixture to the butter mixture and beat just until combined.

Scoop 1 cup of the batter out of the bowl and pour it into a smaller bowl. Add the green tea powder to the cup of batter and stir with a whisk until well blended.

Spoon the "plain" batter alternately with the green tea batter into the prepared pan. Swirl the batters together with a knife. Bake for 60 to 70 minutes, or until golden brown on top and a toothpick inserted in the center comes out clean.

Cool the cake for 20 minutes in the pan. Remove the cake from the pan, peel off the parchment paper, and cool completely on a wire rack.

TO MAKE THE GLAZE, combine the confectioners' sugar and the sake in a small bowl and whisk until smooth. Drizzle over the cake.

Molten Chocolate Orange Cake

MAKES 10 TO 12 SERVINGS

THIS CAKE IS IMPOSSIBLY RICH *and incredibly gooey. Think of it as a full-scale version of the individual chocolate lava cakes so often found on steakhouse menus. While it is irresistible when served warm straight from the oven, the center will stay moist and fudgy overnight so feel free to bake it a day ahead. Store it tented with foil at room temperature. The bracing flavors of the Orange Up cocktail are the perfect complement to the cake's decadent texture. Sip slowly between bites.*

10 ounces bittersweet chocolate, chopped

½ pound (2 sticks) unsalted butter, softened

1¼ cups granulated sugar

6 large eggs, separated

¼ cup orange liqueur, such as Grand Marnier

1 tablespoon freshly grated orange zest (optional)

1 teaspoon pure vanilla extract

1 cup all-purpose flour

¼ teaspoon salt

Confectioners' sugar, for dusting

Preheat the oven to 350°F. Butter a 9-inch springform pan or spray it with nonstick spray. Line the bottom of the pan with parchment paper.

Melt the chocolate in a heatproof bowl set over a pan of simmering water. Set aside to cool slightly.

In a large bowl, beat the butter and 1 cup of the sugar with an electric mixer until light and fluffy, about 2 minutes. Beat in the egg yolks, the orange liqueur, the orange zest (if using), and the vanilla extract. Stir in the melted chocolate. Stir in the flour and salt just until combined.

In another large bowl, beat the egg whites and remaining ¼ cup sugar until soft peaks form, about 4 minutes. Stir one-third of the egg whites into the batter to lighten it. Carefully fold in the remaining egg whites in two additions.

Pour the batter into the prepared pan and bake for 35 to 40 minutes, until the top of the cake is dry and cracked and a toothpick inserted in the side comes out clean, but a toothpick inserted in the center comes out lightly coated with chocolate. Cool the cake slightly; then unmold and dust with confectioners' sugar before serving.

SHAKE IT UP: For a berry version, omit the orange zest and substitute framboise for the orange liqueur.

Orange Up

2 ounces orange liqueur
1 ounce dark rum
½ ounce simple syrup
½ ounce lemon juice
Dash of Angostura bitters
Orange wheel, for garnish

Combine the orange liqueur, rum, simple syrup, lemon juice,
and bitters in a cocktail shaker filled with ice. Shake and strain
into a martini glass. Garnish with the orange wheel.

MAKES
1
DRINK

Plum Biercake

MAKES 6 TO 8 SERVINGS

THIS CAKE IS A GROWN-UP VERSION OF GINGERBREAD *that can be enjoyed at any time of the year. The cinnamon and molasses lend it a festive note that's perfect for the holidays, yet the plums are decidedly summery. Beer, of course, knows no season. Doppelbock is a very strong German lager with a dark color and rich, malty flavor.*

The recipe comes together fast, and the cake will last for up to three days well wrapped on the countertop. Leave a knife nearby for easy snacking.

2 cups all-purpose flour

2 teaspoons ground ginger

2 teaspoons ground cinnamon

1 teaspoon baking soda

¼ teaspoon salt

¼ pound (1 stick) unsalted butter, softened

¾ cup sugar

1 large egg

3 tablespoons molasses

1 cup German doppelbock beer

4 small plums, halved lengthwise, pitted, and cut into wedges

Preheat the oven to 350°F. Grease a 9-inch round baking pan with butter, or spray it with nonstick spray. (A square pan will work too.) Dust the pan with flour and tap out the excess.

In a medium bowl, whisk together the flour, ginger, cinnamon, baking soda, and salt.

In a large bowl, beat the butter and sugar with an electric mixer until light and fluffy, about 2 minutes. Beat in the egg and the molasses. Alternately add the flour mixture and the beer to the butter mixture, beginning and ending with the flour. Beat just until smooth and combined.

Pour the batter into the prepared pan. Arrange the plum wedges in rows on top of the batter. Bake the cake for about 40 minutes, or until a toothpick inserted into the center comes out clean. Cool on a wire rack and then cut into squares and serve.

SHAKE IT UP: Can't find doppelbock? Substitute another dark, richly flavored beer, such as a porter or stout.

Coffee Maple Walnut Cake

MAKES 8 SERVINGS

THIS CAKE TASTES A LITTLE BIT LIKE PANCAKES. *Add coffee liqueur and you've got a complete, boozy brunch. Because I'm from New England, I'm a purist when it comes to maple syrup—only the real thing will do. Don't be tempted to substitute the artificial stuff. This is a great recipe to make ahead, as the flavors intensify overnight.*

FOR THE CAKE:

2 cups (about 8 ounces) finely ground walnuts

1 cup all-purpose flour

1 teaspoon baking powder

¼ teaspoon salt

¼ pound (1 stick) unsalted butter, softened

1 cup sugar

3 large eggs, separated

1 teaspoon pure vanilla extract

½ cup milk

FOR THE COFFEE MAPLE SYRUP:

¼ cup sugar

¼ cup maple syrup

⅓ cup coffee liqueur

2 tablespoons water

Preheat the oven to 350°F. Grease a 9-inch springform pan with butter, or spray it with nonstick spray. Dust the pan with flour and tap out the excess.

TO MAKE THE WALNUT CAKE, whisk together the walnuts, flour, baking powder, and salt in a medium bowl.

In a large bowl, beat the butter and sugar with an electric mixer until light and fluffy, about 2 minutes. Add the egg yolks, one at a time, beating after each addition. Beat in the vanilla. Add the dry ingredients alternately with the milk, beginning and ending with the flour and beating well after each addition. Wash and dry the beaters.

In a large bowl, beat the egg whites until they hold stiff peaks. Gently fold the egg whites into the batter.

Pour the batter into the prepared pan and gently smooth the surface with a spatula. Bake for 30 to 40 minutes, or until a toothpick inserted into the center comes out clean. Set the pan on a wire rack to cool.

TO MAKE THE COFFEE MAPLE SYRUP, combine the sugar, maple syrup, coffee liqueur, and water in a small saucepan. Bring to a boil over medium heat. Reduce the heat to medium low and simmer the syrup until it thickens slightly, 3 to 5 minutes.

Pour half the warm syrup over the cake in the pan. Let the cake stand for at least 1 hour before serving to allow the syrup to really soak into it. Serve with the remaining syrup.

SHAKE IT UP: For a totally nutty version, substitute walnut liqueur.

Devilish Angel Food Cake

MAKES 8 TO 10 SERVINGS

ANGEL FOOD CAKE IS OFTEN TOUTED FOR BEING *low in fat and therefore sin free. I can't speak for everyone, but "healthy" isn't really a characteristic I look for in dessert. This version of angel food cake, laced with cocoa and spiked with cinnamon schnapps, is downright devilish. Scrumptious and fluffy, it's perfect for hot summer nights when topped with scoops of raspberry or chocolate sorbet. It sounds strange, but it's important to allow angel food cakes to cool upside down. Otherwise, they won't come out of the pan properly.*

FOR THE CAKE:

1¼ cups confectioners' sugar

1 cup cake flour

½ teaspoon ground cinnamon

¼ teaspoon salt

12 large egg whites, at room temperature

1½ teaspoons cream of tartar

1 cup granulated sugar

2 teaspoons cinnamon schnapps

2 tablespoons cocoa powder

FOR THE CINNAMON SCHNAPPS GLAZE:

1 cup confectioners' sugar

2 tablespoons cinnamon schnapps

Preheat the oven to 350°F.

TO MAKE THE CAKE, sift together the confectioners' sugar, flour, cinnamon, and salt in a large bowl. Resift a second time, and set aside.

In another large bowl, combine the egg whites and cream of tartar. Beat with an electric mixer on high speed until they form soft peaks, 2 to 3 minutes. Gradually add the granulated sugar and continue beating until thick and shiny. Add the cinnamon schnapps and beat to combine.

Working in four additions, gently fold the flour mixture into the egg white mixture until just incorporated.

Ladle out 1 cup of the batter and place it in a small bowl. Sprinkle the cocoa powder over the batter and fold in gently, just until combined.

Alternately spoon the plain batter and the chocolate batter into an ungreased 10-inch tube pan. Swirl the batters together with a butter knife. Transfer the pan to the oven and bake 35 to 40 minutes, or until the top is golden brown and the cake springs back when pressed lightly. Invert the cake over a wine bottle or on a rack and allow it to cool completely before removing it from the pan.

TO MAKE THE CINNAMON SCHNAPPS GLAZE, combine the confectioners' sugar with the cinnamon schnapps in a small bowl and whisk until smooth. Drizzle over the cooled cake.

SHAKE IT UP: Substitute cinnamon-flavored vodka for the cinnamon schnapps.

Individual Raspberry-
Almond Cheesecakes

JUNIOR'S, THE BROOKLYN CHEESECAKE INSTITUTION, *makes adorable mini cheesecakes called "little fellas." They are decidedly delicious, but they lack a graham cracker crust, which is my favorite part, so I decided to come up with my own version.*

These cheesecakes are so tiny and adorable that it's hard to believe they pack in not one, but two kinds of booze. It's possible that when you prepare them you will end up with a bit of extra batter. I say, all the better for when it's time to lick the bowl!

FOR THE CRUST:

1 cup finely ground
  graham cracker crumbs

¼ cup sugar

4 tablespoons unsalted
  butter, melted

FOR THE FILLING:

2 (8-ounce) packages
  cream cheese, at room
  temperature

¾ cup sugar

1 tablespoon cornstarch

¼ cup almond liqueur, such
  as amaretto

2 large eggs

¼ cup sour cream

1 (½-pint) container fresh
  raspberries

1½ tablespoons framboise

Preheat the oven to 350°F. Line a 12-cup standard muffin pan with paper liners.

TO MAKE THE CRUST, in a small bowl, combine the graham cracker crumbs, sugar, and melted butter. Toss with a fork until well blended.

Drop a few heaping spoonfuls of the graham cracker mixture into the bottom of each muffin cup and pack it down gently with your fingers. Bake 5 minutes. Remove the pan from the oven and allow the crusts to cool while you prepare the filling. Do not turn the oven off.

TO MAKE THE FILLING, using an electric mixer, beat the cream cheese, sugar, and cornstarch until smooth. Add the almond liqueur, eggs, and sour cream and beat until smooth. Set aside.

Reserve 12 raspberries. Purée the remaining raspberries and framboise in a blender until smooth. Fill muffin cups two-thirds full with the cream cheese mixture and drop generous teaspoonful of the raspberry purée on top. With a toothpick, create a swirled pattern on top.

Place the muffin pan in a large, shallow roasting pan with enough hot water to come about 1 inch up the sides of the pan. Bake until the cakes are puffy and barely set in the center, 35 to 40 minutes.

When done, allow to cool for 2 hours. Transfer the cheesecakes, still in the pan, to the refrigerator and chill for at least 4 hours or overnight.

To serve the cheesecakes, remove each one from the pan and garnish with a reserved raspberry.

SHAKE IT UP: Substitute hazelnut liqueur for framboise.

"Bottoms Up" Pineapple-Tequila Cake

MAKES 8 TO 10 SERVINGS

WHO DOESN'T SMILE SHEEPISHLY AT *the old George Carlin quote, "one tequila, two tequila, three tequila, floor"? I certainly learned the hard way that a little tequila can go a very, very long way. Fortunately, good tequila is as flavorful as it is alcoholic. This cake contains only three tablespoons of booze, but it packs a wallop of tequila taste. A big piece will leave you stuffed, but happily hangover free.*

FOR THE PINEAPPLE TOPPING:

- 4 tablespoons (½ stick) unsalted butter
- ⅔ cup packed light brown sugar
- 1 tablespoon gold tequila
- ½ small pineapple, peeled, quartered, and sliced

FOR THE CAKE:

- 1½ cups all-purpose flour
- 1½ teaspoons baking powder
- ¼ teaspoon salt
- ¼ teaspoon ground cinnamon
- 6 tablespoons (¾ stick) unsalted butter, softened
- ¾ cup sugar
- 2 large eggs
- 2 tablespoons gold tequila
- ¾ cup well-shaken buttermilk

Preheat the oven to 350°F.

TO MAKE THE PINEAPPLE TOPPING, place a 9-inch nonstick metal cake pan on the stovetop over low heat. Add the butter to the pan and let it melt, stirring occasionally. Add the brown sugar and the tequila and cook, stirring constantly, until the mixture is smooth and thick, 4 to 5 minutes. Remove the pan from the heat and arrange the pineapple slices over the sugar mixture. Set aside.

TO MAKE THE CAKE, whisk the flour, baking powder, salt, and cinnamon together in a medium bowl.

In a large bowl, beat the butter and sugar with an electric mixer until light and fluffy, about 2 minutes. Add the eggs, one at a time, beating well after each addition. Beat in the tequila. Add the flour mixture alternately with the buttermilk, beginning and ending with the flour and beating just until incorporated after each addition.

Pour the batter into the pan over the pineapple. Bake until the cake is set and golden and a toothpick inserted in the center comes out clean, about 45 minutes.

Cool the cake in the pan for 15 minutes and then run a knife around the edges. Set a plate upside down over the cake and flip the cake, inverting it onto the plate. Serve the cake warm or at room temperature.

SHAKE IT UP: Substitute dark rum for the tequila.

Brandied Pear Cake with White Chocolate Chunks

WHEN I WAS IN GRADUATE SCHOOL, *I was a waitress at a popular Italian trattoria in Brooklyn. At the end of the night, we each got to have a glass of wine and, if we were lucky, a piece of yesterday's chocolate-pear cake, which was the restaurant's signature dessert.*

I never managed to get my hands on the chef's recipe, but I've done my best to reinvent it here, substituting white chocolate for the dark, and—in honor of that much loved and much needed shift drink—a healthy dose of brandy.

FOR THE BRANDIED PEARS:

2 tablespoons sugar

¼ cup brandy

2 teaspoons freshly squeezed lemon juice

2 medium-firm, ripe pears, peeled, cored, and cut into ½-inch chunks (about 2 cups)

FOR THE CAKE:

1 cup all-purpose flour

1 tablespoon baking powder

¼ teaspoon salt

¼ pound (1 stick) unsalted butter

3 large eggs

⅔ cup sugar

½ cup chopped white chocolate or white chocolate chips

TO MAKE THE BRANDIED PEARS, combine the sugar, brandy, and lemon juice in a medium bowl. Add the pears and stir to coat. Allow the pears to macerate for 20 minutes, and then strain them over a small bowl. Set the pears aside. Reserve the brandy mixture.

TO MAKE THE CAKE, preheat the oven to 350°F. Grease a 9-inch springform pan with butter, or spray it with nonstick spray. Dust with flour and tap out the excess.

In a medium bowl, whisk together the flour, baking powder, and salt.

In a small saucepan, melt the butter over low heat. Cook for 8 to 10 minutes, or until the butter begins to brown and develops a nutty aroma. (Don't be alarmed by how much the butter foams—it's supposed to happen!) Remove the butter from the heat.

In a large bowl, beat the eggs with an electric mixer at high speed until very light and thick, about 5 minutes. Gradually add the sugar and beat for 2 minutes until fully incorporated.

Turn the electric mixer to low speed and add 1 tablespoon of the reserved brandy mixture, saving the rest of the brandy mixture for the Brandied Pear Belinis (La Pera Prosecco cocktails). Alternately add the flour mixture and the browned butter to the egg mixture, beginning and ending with the flour. Beat until just barely combined.

Pour the batter into the prepared pan. Top with the pears and white chocolate chunks. Bake until the cake is golden brown and a toothpick inserted in the center comes out clean, about 45 minutes. Cool completely in the pan and then release the sides and serve.

SHAKE IT UP: Substitute bourbon for the brandy, or for added flavor, substitute orange juice for the lemon juice and orange liqueur, such as Grand Marnier, for the brandy.

Brandied Pear Belinis

MAKES
6
COCKTAILS

Reserved brandy mixture from Brandied Pear Cake
with White Chocolate Chunks
One 750-ml bottle Prosecco
Twists of fresh orange or lemon peel, for garnish

Divide the brandy mixture among six Champagne flutes.
Top with Prosecco and garnish with a twist.

Pumpkin Pomegranate Layer Cake

POMEGRANATE JUICE MAY BE INCREDIBLY HEALTHY, *but I think pomegranate liqueur is much more fun. The most widely available brand, Pama, is a potent blend of pomegranate juice, vodka, and tequila. Its ruby red color makes for exotic cocktails—and festive frostings. Pomegranate season runs from September to January, so this cake is perfect for the holidays.*

MAKES 12 TO 16 SERVINGS

FOR THE CAKE:

2 cups all-purpose flour

1 teaspoon baking soda

1 teaspoon baking powder

1 teaspoon ground cinnamon

½ teaspoon salt

½ teaspoon ground ginger

½ teaspoon ground nutmeg

1 cup granulated sugar

1 cup packed dark brown sugar

½ cup vegetable oil

3 large eggs

1 (15-ounce) can pumpkin purée (not pumpkin pie mix)

FOR THE FROSTING:

14 tablespoons (1¾ sticks) unsalted butter, softened

6 to 8 cups confectioners' sugar

¼ cup milk

¼ cup pomegranate liqueur, such as Pama

1 cup pomegranate seeds (from 1 medium pomegranate)

Preheat the oven to 350°F. Grease two 8-inch round cake pans with butter or nonstick spray. Dust them with flour and tap out the excess.

TO MAKE THE CAKE, combine the flour, baking soda, baking powder, cinnamon, salt, ginger, and nutmeg in a medium bowl.

In a large bowl, combine both sugars and the oil. Beat with an electric mixer until well blended, about 2 minutes. Beat in the eggs, one at a time, and then beat in the pumpkin purée.

Gradually add the flour mixture to the oil mixture and beat until just combined. Divide the batter between the prepared pans and bake for 30 to 35 minutes, or until a toothpick comes out clean. Cool the cakes for 10 minutes in the pans, and then remove the cakes from the pans and allow them to cool completely on a wire rack.

TO MAKE THE FROSTING, beat the butter in a large bowl with an electric mixer for about 2 minutes. Add 6 cups of the confectioners' sugar, the milk, and the pomegranate liqueur. Beat on low speed until creamy. Gradually add the remaining confectioners' sugar, a little at a time, until it reaches desired consistency.

Place one cake layer on a plate and spread it with about one-third of the frosting. Sprinkle with ½ cup pomegranate seeds. Top with the remaining cake layer and spread the remaining frosting over the top and sides. Sprinkle with the remaining pomegranate seeds.

SHAKE IT UP: Substitute hazelnut liqueur, such as Frangelico, for the pomegranate liqueur, and chopped toasted hazelnuts for the pomegranate seeds.

Jägermeister and Honey Bundt Cake

MAKES 10 TO 12 SERVINGS

CONTRARY TO THE PERSISTENT URBAN LEGEND, Jägermeister does not, in fact, contain the blood of an elk or a deer. This German digestif is made from a blend of more than fifty herbs and spices and has a semisweet flavor reminiscent of licorice. It's definitely a soul-warming kind of booze, perfect for this dense, hearty Bundt cake. This recipe is courtesy of cookbook author extraordinaire Rick Rodgers, a friend and culinary mentor of mine. His original version uses Drambuie, a honey and herb-flavored whisky, and is equally delicious.

FOR THE CAKE:

2¼ cups all-purpose flour

2 teaspoons baking soda

2 teaspoons ground ginger

2 teaspoons ground cinnamon

½ teaspoon ground cloves

½ teaspoon salt

½ pound (2 sticks) unsalted butter, softened

1 cup packed light brown sugar

2 large eggs

1 cup honey

½ cup Jägermeister

¾ cup hot water

FOR THE GLAZE:

4 tablespoons (½ stick) unsalted butter

⅓ cup Jägermeister

Confectioners' sugar, for dusting

Preheat the oven to 350°F. Grease a 12-cup nonstick Bundt pan with butter, or spray it with nonstick spray. Dust with flour and tap out the excess.

TO MAKE THE CAKE, combine the flour, baking soda, ginger, cinnamon, cloves, and salt in a medium bowl.

In a large bowl, beat the butter with the brown sugar until well combined, about 1 minute. Beat in the eggs one at a time, and then beat in the honey and the Jägermeister. Stir the flour mixture into the butter mixture with a wooden spoon just until well combined. Stir in the hot water. Pour the batter into the prepared pan and smooth the top.

Bake the cake 45 to 50 minutes, or until a toothpick inserted in the center comes out clean. Remove the cake from the oven and cool in the pan on a wire rack for 15 minutes.

TO MAKE THE GLAZE, melt the butter in a small saucepan over low heat. Remove the saucepan from the heat and stir in the Jägermeister. Brush the top of the cake (while it is still in the pan) with 2 tablespoons of the glaze. Allow the cake to stand for 5 minutes.

Turn the cake out onto a serving plate, brush with the remaining glaze, and allow it to cool completely. Dust with confectioners' sugar before serving.

SHAKE IT UP: Substitute another herbal liqueur, such as Bénédictine or Chartreuse, for the Jägermeister.

Honey Bear
Cocktail

2¹/₂ ounces milk

1 ounce Jägermeister

1 ounce coffee liqueur, such as Kahlùa

1 ounce honey liqueur, such as Bärenjäger,
Krupnik, or Wild Turkey American Honey

Mix all ingredients in a shaker. Serve over ice.

MAKES
1
DRINK

Champagne Layer Cake

MAKES
12
SERVINGS

MY EARLIEST EXPERIENCES WITH CHAMPAGNE involved mixing large quantities of J. Rogét with orange juice in red plastic cups to make "mimosas." Classy, huh? No wonder I couldn't understand what all the fuss was about. I didn't get a taste of the real thing until much later, when friends celebrating their engagement poured me a flute of Dom Pérignon. What a revelation! Now I would use Champagne instead of milk on my breakfast cereal, if only it wouldn't garner such strange looks.

This cake is a great way to incorporate more bubbly into your life. Despite the fact that it sounds like the epitome of decadence, it's actually quite light. Make it for birthdays, for New Year's Eve, or on a random Saturday afternoon, just because.

FOR THE CAKE:

1¼ cups all-purpose flour

1 cup cake flour

2 teaspoons baking powder

¼ teaspoon salt

10 tablespoons (1 stick plus 2 tablespoons) unsalted butter, softened

1 cup sugar

⅔ cup Champagne

5 large egg whites

FOR THE BUTTERCREAM FROSTING:

¼ pound (1 stick) unsalted butter, softened

3 to 4 cups confectioners' sugar

1 tablespoon milk

3 tablespoons Champagne

Preheat the oven to 350°F. Grease two 9-inch round cake pans with butter, or spray them with nonstick spray. Dust with flour and tap out the excess.

TO MAKE THE CAKE, whisk together the all-purpose flour, cake flour, baking powder, and salt in a medium bowl.

In a large bowl, beat the butter with the sugar until light and fluffy, about 2 minutes. Alternately add the flour mixture and the Champagne to the butter mixture, beginning and ending with the flour, and beating well after each addition.

In another large bowl, beat the egg whites with an electric mixer until stiff peaks form. Whisk a generous spoonful of the beaten egg whites into the Champagne batter to lighten it. Then carefully fold the remaining egg whites into the batter with a spatula.

Divide the batter between the prepared cake pans and bake for 25 to 30 minutes, or until a toothpick inserted into the center comes out clean and the tops of the cakes spring back when pressed lightly.

Let the cakes cool for 15 minutes in the pans, and then remove them and allow to cool completely on a wire rack.

TO MAKE THE BUTTERCREAM FROSTING, combine the butter and 2 cups of the confectioners' sugar in a medium bowl. Beat with an electric mixer until smooth and creamy, about 3 minutes. Beat in the milk and Champagne. With the mixer running, gradually add 1 to 2 more cups of confectioners' sugar until the buttercream is thick and creamy.

Place one cake layer on a plate and spread with half of the buttercream frosting. Top with the remaining cake layer and spread with the remaining frosting.

SHAKE IT UP: Substitute Prosecco or cava for the Champagne.

Southern Peach

1 sugar cube
2 dashes Angostura bitters
½ ounce bourbon
½ ounce peach schnapps
Champagne (or other dry sparkling wine)
Maraschino cherry (optional)

Drop the sugar cube into the bottom of a Champagne flute and add the bitters. Allow them to soak for a minute or two; then put in the bourbon and peach schnapps. Top with Champagne and garnish with the cherry.

MAKES
1
DRINK

Lemon Layer Cake with Campari Frosting

MY FAVORITE MOVIE FROM THE 1980s *is* Big Business. *In it, Bette Midler orders a Campari and soda at the Plaza Hotel and tells the waiter to "make it snappy." It's a hilarious scene, and one of the first times Campari—an herbaceous Italian digestif—was mentioned in mainstream American media. Since Campari is very bitter, I've mixed it with sweeter limoncello in this bright, citrus cake that is perfect for spring.*

MAKES 12 SERVINGS

FOR THE CAKE:

1½ cups all-purpose flour

1 cup cake flour

1 teaspoon baking powder

½ teaspoon baking soda

¼ teaspoon salt

¼ pound (1 stick) unsalted butter, softened

1¼ cups granulated sugar

3 large eggs

¾ cup buttermilk

2 tablespoons limoncello

2 tablespoons freshly squeezed lemon juice

1 tablespoon grated lemon zest

FOR THE CAMPARI BUTTERCREAM FROSTING:

¼ pound (1 stick) unsalted butter, softened

3 to 4 cups confectioners' sugar

1 tablespoon milk

2 tablespoons limoncello

1 tablespoon Campari

Preheat the oven to 350°F. Grease two 8-inch round cake pans with butter, or spray them with nonstick spray. Line the bottoms with parchment paper. Dust the pans with flour and tap out the excess.

TO MAKE THE CAKE, whisk the all-purpose flour, cake flour, baking powder, baking soda, and salt in a medium bowl.

In a large bowl, beat the butter and sugar with an electric mixer until light and fluffy, about 3 minutes. Add the eggs one at a time, beating after each addition.

Alternately add the flour mixture and the buttermilk to the butter mixture, beginning and ending with the flour, and beating well after each addition. Add the limoncello, lemon juice, and lemon zest and beat just until incorporated.

Divide the batter between the two prepared pans and bake for 30 minutes, or until the cakes are puffed and a toothpick inserted into the center comes out clean. Cool the cakes 10 minutes in the pans, and then remove and cool completely on a wire rack.

TO MAKE THE FROSTING, beat the butter and 2 cups of the confectioners' sugar with an electric mixer about 3 minutes. Beat in the milk, limoncello, and Campari. Gradually beat in 1 to 2 more cups of confectioners' sugar until buttercream is thick and creamy.

Place one cake layer on a plate and spread with half of the buttercream. Top with the remaining cake layer and spread with the remaining buttercream.

SHAKE IT UP: Substitute cherry liqueur, such as kirsch, for the Campari and add a drop or two of red food coloring to the frosting.

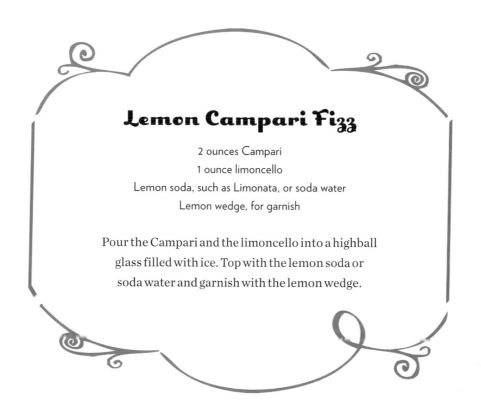

Lemon Campari Fizz

2 ounces Campari

1 ounce limoncello

Lemon soda, such as Limonata, or soda water

Lemon wedge, for garnish

Pour the Campari and the limoncello into a highball
glass filled with ice. Top with the lemon soda or
soda water and garnish with the lemon wedge.

MAKES
1
DRINK

Southern Comfort Red Velvet Cake

MAKES 12 TO 16 SERVINGS OR 24 CUPCAKES

SAY "SOUTHERN COMFORT" AND MOST PEOPLE *will roll their eyes and groan, "SoCo. I haven't had that since college." It's true that this sugary whiskey is a dorm room staple, along with John Belushi posters and economy-size plastic kegs of pretzels. But SoCo's often-mocked sweetness lends itself to baking, yielding a subtle hint of whiskey without overpowering the other flavors. What could be more Southern or comforting than incorporating it into red velvet cake?*

FOR THE CAKE:

3 cups cake flour

4 tablespoons cocoa powder

1½ teaspoons baking soda

½ teaspoon salt

¾ cup buttermilk

¼ cup Southern Comfort

1 teaspoon pure vanilla extract

1 teaspoon white vinegar

1 (1-ounce) bottle red food coloring

12 tablespoons (1½ sticks) unsalted butter, softened

2 cups granulated sugar

3 large eggs

FOR THE FROSTING:

14 tablespoons (1¾ sticks) unsalted butter, softened

6 to 8 cups confectioners' sugar

¼ cup milk

¼ cup Southern Comfort

Chopped toasted pecans, for garnish (optional)

Preheat the oven to 350°F. Grease two 9-inch round cake pans with butter or nonstick spray. Dust with flour and tap out the excess.

TO MAKE THE CAKE, whisk together the cake flour, cocoa powder, baking soda, and salt. In a separate bowl, whisk together the buttermilk, Southern Comfort, vanilla, vinegar, and food coloring.

In a large bowl, beat the butter and sugar with an electric mixer for 2 to 3 minutes. Add the eggs, one at a time, beating well after each addition. Add the flour mixture alternately with the milk mixture in three additions, beginning and ending with the flour.

Divide the batter between the prepared pans and bake for 30 to 40 minutes, or until a toothpick inserted in the center of the cakes comes out clean. Let the cakes cool in the pans on a wire rack, and then remove them from the pans and cool completely.

TO MAKE THE FROSTING, beat the butter in a large bowl with an electric mixer for about 2 minutes. Add 6 cups of the confectioners' sugar, the milk, and the Southern Comfort. Beat on low speed until creamy. Gradually add the remaining confectioners' sugar, a little at a time, until the frosting has reached the desired consistency.

Place one cake layer on a plate and spread it with about one-third of the frosting. Top with the remaining cake layer and spread the remaining frosting over the top and sides of the cake. Sprinkle the cake with chopped pecans, if using.

SHAKE IT UP: For a bolder flavor, substitute Tennessee whiskey, such as Jack Daniels, for the Southern Comfort.

Sachertorte

For a long time I thought a Sachertorte *was impossibly fussy and fancy. It was the sort of dessert a person bought at an elegant bakery filled with burnished old mirrors and workers in puffy white hats, not something thrown together in the kitchen at home. But actually, this Austrian confection is easy to bake, and the results never fail to impress. It would make a truly elegant holiday dessert—and a much welcome alternative to those dreaded fruitcakes.*

FOR THE TORTE:

5 ounces bittersweet chocolate, chopped

¼ pound (1 stick) unsalted butter, softened

1 cup sugar, divided

6 large eggs, separated

1 tablespoon apricot brandy

1 cup all-purpose flour

FOR THE APRICOT GLAZE:

1 cup apricot preserves

3 tablespoons apricot brandy

FOR THE CHOCOLATE GLAZE:

5 ounces bittersweet chocolate, chopped

½ cup heavy cream

4 tablespoons unsalted butter

2 tablespoons apricot brandy

Preheat the oven to 350°F. Grease two 8-inch round cake pans with butter, or spray with nonstick spray. Line the bottoms of the pans with parchment paper. Dust with flour and tap out the excess.

TO MAKE THE TORTE, place the chocolate in a heatproof bowl and set the bowl over a pan of simmering water. Heat, stirring occasionally, until the chocolate is melted and smooth. Remove the bowl from the heat and allow the chocolate to cool to room temperature.

In a large bowl, beat the butter and ¾ cup of the sugar with an electric mixer until very light and fluffy, about 3 minutes. Beat in the egg yolks, one at a time, scraping down the sides of the bowl as needed. Beat in the apricot brandy and the cooled chocolate. Set aside. Wash and dry the beaters.

In another large bowl, beat the egg whites with the remaining ¼ cup sugar until they form soft peaks. Stir one-third of the beaten whites into the chocolate mixture to lighten it, and then carefully fold in the remaining whites until only a few streaks of white remain. Sprinkle ½ cup of the flour over the batter and fold in until incorporated. Repeat with the remaining ½ cup flour.

Divide the batter between the two cake pans and bake for about 20 minutes, or until cakes are puffed and a toothpick inserted into the center comes out clean. Remove the cakes from the oven and allow to cool on a wire rack for 15 minutes. Run a knife around the edge of each pan and invert each cake over a plate. Peel off the parchment paper.

(continued on next page)

TO MAKE THE APRICOT GLAZE, bring the apricot preserves and apricot brandy to a boil in a medium saucepan over medium heat. Reduce the heat to a simmer, and cook until mixture is thickened, about 5 minutes. Remove from heat and set aside.

Place one torte layer on a plate lined with two pieces of waxed paper (align them so that each piece covers half the plate and they overlap slightly in the middle). Spread the torte layer with half of the apricot jam mixture. Top with the remaining torte layer, and spread with the remaining jam mixture. Let stand while you make the chocolate glaze.

TO MAKE THE CHOCOLATE GLAZE, place the chopped chocolate in a small mixing bowl. Heat the heavy cream in a small saucepan over low heat until it reaches a simmer. Pour the heated cream over the chocolate. Let stand 2 minutes and then stir until smooth. Stir in the butter until smooth. Stir in the apricot brandy.

Immediately pour the glaze over the cake. Using an offset spatula, smooth the glaze over the top and sides of the torte, making sure to cover it completely. Refrigerate the cake until the glaze is set, about 1 hour. Gently pull the sheets of wax paper out from underneath it, cut the torte into thin wedges, and serve.

SHAKE IT UP: Substitute orange marmalade for the apricot jam, and orange liqueur for the apricot brandy.

"Can't Say Nocello" Carrot Cake Cupcakes

MAKES 12 to 16 SERVINGS OR 24 CUPCAKES

IS THERE A BETTER WAY TO EAT YOUR VEGETABLES *than by devouring a spicy carrot cupcake topped with a slick of cream cheese frosting? I doubt it. When it comes to carrot cake there are endless variations: Some include pineapple, others raisins, still others coconut. Since I've always liked walnut versions best, I decided to enhance this recipe with a nip of Nocello, a walnut-flavored liqueur from the Emiligia-Romagna region of Italy. If you prefer fruit to nuts, reduce the walnuts to one-fourth cup and add one-half cup raisins or diced pineapple.*

FOR THE CUPCAKES:

2 cups all-purpose flour

2 teaspoons baking soda

¾ teaspoon salt

1 teaspoon ground cinnamon

¾ teaspoon ground ginger

¼ teaspoon ground nutmeg

1 cup granulated sugar

1 cup canola oil

¼ cup walnut liqueur, such as Nocello

3 large eggs

3 cups peeled, grated carrots (slightly less than 1 pound)

¾ cup chopped walnuts

FOR THE CREAM CHEESE FROSTING:

1 (8-ounce) package cream cheese, softened

3 tablespoons unsalted butter, softened

1 to 2 cups confectioners' sugar

2 tablespoons walnut liqueur

Preheat the oven to 350°F. Line two 12-cup muffin pans with paper liners.

TO MAKE THE CUPCAKES, whisk the flour, baking soda, salt, cinnamon, ginger, and nutmeg in a medium bowl.

In a large bowl, whisk the sugar with the canola oil and the walnut liqueur. Whisk in the eggs, one at a time. Add the flour mixture and whisk until blended. Then stir in the carrots and walnuts.

Scoop the batter into the muffin cups, filling each three-fourths full. Bake the cupcakes until a toothpick inserted in the center comes out clean and the tops spring back when pressed lightly, 18 to 20 minutes. Cool the cupcakes in the pans for 5 minutes. Then remove them from the pan and cool them completely on a wire rack.

TO MAKE THE CREAM CHEESE FROSTING, place the cream cheese in a medium bowl and beat with an electric mixer for 2 minutes, or until it is slightly softened. Add the butter and beat until combined. Add 1 cup of the confectioners' sugar and beat until smooth. With the mixer running, gradually add the remaining cup of confectioners' sugar, if needed, until the frosting is smooth and thick. Add the walnut liqueur and beat until incorporated. Spread the frosting over the cooled cupcakes.

SHAKE IT UP: Substitute almond or hazelnut liqueur for the walnut liqueur.

Lavender Honey-Nut Cupcakes

I THINK LAVENDER TASTES LIKE SOAP IN A GOOD WAY: *delicate, clean, and floral. These cupcakes are incredibly pretty, especially when sprinkled with dried lavender buds. Serve them at your next tea party. By which I mean, your next Long Island Iced Tea party. Dried lavender buds can be difficult to find. I order mine online from Kalustyans.com.*

FOR THE CUPCAKES:

1¼ cups all-purpose flour

¼ cup almond meal or finely ground almonds

1 teaspoon dried lavender buds

1 teaspoon baking powder

¼ teaspoon salt

¼ pound (1 stick) unsalted butter, softened

1 cup granulated sugar

2 large eggs

¼ cup half-and-half or milk

¼ cup almond liqueur, such as amaretto

FOR THE FROSTING:

6 tablespoons (¾ stick) unsalted butter, softened

3 to 4 cups confectioners' sugar

3 tablespoons honey

2 tablespoons half-and-half or milk

2 tablespoons almond liqueur, such as amaretto

Dried lavender buds, for garnish

Preheat the oven to 350°F. Line a 12-cup muffin pan with paper liners.

TO MAKE THE CUPCAKES, whisk the flour, almond meal, lavender buds, baking powder, and salt in a small bowl.

In a large bowl, beat the butter and sugar with an electric mixer until light and fluffy, about 3 minutes. Add the eggs, one at a time, beating well after each addition.

Combine the half-and-half and the almond liqueur in a liquid measuring cup. Alternately add the flour mixture and the milk mixture to the butter mixture, beginning and ending with the flour mixture, beating just until incorporated after each addition.

Divide the batter between the muffin cups, filling each two-thirds full. Bake 20 to 25 minutes, or until the tops of the cupcakes spring back when pressed lightly and a toothpick inserted into the center comes out clean. Cool the cupcakes in the pan for 10 minutes, and then remove them and allow to cool completely on a wire rack.

TO MAKE THE FROSTING, combine the butter and 2 cups of confectioners' sugar in a large bowl. Beat with an electric mixer until smooth and creamy, about 3 minutes. Add the honey, half-and-half, and almond liqueur, and beat until incorporated. Gradually beat in another 1 to 2 cups of the confectioners' sugar until the frosting is thick and creamy.

Spread the frosting over the cooled cupcakes and sprinkle with dried lavender buds, if using.

SHAKE IT UP: Substitute finely ground walnuts for the almond meal, and walnut liqueur, such as Nocello, for the almond liqueur. Or, substitute honey liqueur, such as Bärenjäger, for the almond liqueur.

NOTE: To make a 9-inch layer cake, grease two 9-inch round cake pans with butter or spray them with nonstick spray. Line the bottoms with parchment paper, and butter or spray the paper. Dust with flour and tap out the excess. Divide the batter between the pans and bake for 35 to 40 minutes, or until a toothpick inserted in the center comes out clean. Cool the cakes in the pans for 20 minutes. Then remove them from the pan and cool completely on a wire rack. Prepare a double batch of the frosting. Place one cake layer on a serving plate and spread with one-third of the frosting. Top with the remaining cake layer. Spread the remaining frosting over the top of the cake and around the sides.

Almond Iced Tea

5 black tea bags, preferably orange pekoe
6 cups cold water, divided
1 cup almond liqueur, such as amaretto
1 lemon, cut into 8 wedges

Place the tea bags in a large heatproof pitcher. Bring 4 cups of the water to a boil in a saucepan or pot. Pour the boiling water over the tea bags and allow the tea to steep for 1 hour. Remove the tea bags and stir in the remaining 2 cups of cold water and the almond liqueur. Serve over ice, garnished with a lemon slice.

MAKES
8
DRINKS

PiES AND TARTS
À LA BOOZE

A **few years ago, just before Thanksgiving,** my friend Bryan and I attended a lecture and demonstration at the Brooklyn Public Library about holiday pies. More specifically, it was about how to make the perfect piecrust. Subjects addressed included the importance of cold butter and ice water, the merits of food processors versus old-fashioned pastry cutters, pie weights versus beans, and different crimping techniques for the edges. At the end of the demonstration, everyone in the audience (me, Bryan, and about a hundred little old ladies) got a sample of pie in a little paper cup.

It was all very inspiring. So inspiring, in fact, that on Thanksgiving morning I decided to deviate from the tried-and-true piecrust I've been making for years and try out the recipe from the demonstration. Disaster ensued. Ten minutes into the baking time, the edges of the dough melted off my beautiful apple pie and began to smolder and burn in a puddle on the bottom of the oven. I ended up serving the pie with "the crusts cut off," like a child's peanut butter and jelly sandwich.

Was it a bad recipe? I don't think so. In retrospect, I believe I just didn't let the dough chill long enough. But my point in relaying the story is this: When it comes to making perfect piecrusts, don't stress over the minor details. Just learn what works best for you and stick to it.

The piecrust I use is an amalgamation of two recipes, one from *Bon Appetit* and one from *Cook's Illustrated*. The former has the perfect ratio of flour, butter, and water, while the latter incorporates a bit of alcohol for flaky results. I played around with both recipes for years until I finally reached a quick, easy, and foolproof version that I'm completely married to and use for all my pies.

But because the prospect of making piecrust from scratch can be more than a little daunting (especially for novice home bakers), I've also included a number of recipes in this chapter for pies and tarts with graham cracker, cookie, and press-in crusts. The fillings are sauced with assertive or sweet alcohols, such as scotch or framboise, which stand up to flavorful fruits and complex chocolate. Some recipes are perfect for holiday feasts, such as Hard Cider Apple Pie and Cranberry, Chocolate, and Pecan Pie, while others—like the Rustic Fig Galette and the Plum and Hazelnut Tart—are perfect for casual cookouts in the summer months.

A final note: All pies are better served à la mode. And à la booze!

Hard Cider Apple Pie

MAKES 8 SERVINGS

MY MOTHER AND I LIKE RAISINS IN OUR APPLE PIE, *but my father and my brother don't. I have a vivid childhood memory of watching my mom divide a bowl of sliced apples in half, add raisins to one, and then pour them both side by side into a piecrust. She's a genius, I thought. Like whoever invented half-cheese, half-pepperoni pizza.*

This recipe is a boozy take on apple cider pie, a classic New England dessert made by simmering apples in cider before pouring them into the crust. I've left out the raisins, but you can certainly stir in half a cup with the lemon zest if you prefer.

FOR THE CRUST:

2½ cups all-purpose flour

2 tablespoons granulated sugar

½ teaspoon salt

¼ pound plus 4 tablespoons (1½ sticks) unsalted butter, well chilled and cut into ½-inch cubes

1 tablespoon vodka

6 to 8 tablespoons ice water

2 tablespoons heavy cream

1 tablespoon raw sugar (optional)

FOR THE FILLING:

2½ pounds (about 5 medium) Granny Smith apples, peeled, cored, and cut into ¾-inch slices

⅔ cup plus 2 tablespoons hard cider, divided

⅓ cup packed dark brown sugar

⅓ cup granulated sugar

¾ teaspoon ground cinnamon

TO MAKE THE CRUST, combine the flour, sugar, and salt in the work bowl of a food processor. Give it a few good pulses to combine. Add the cubes of butter, a few at a time, and pulse until the mixture looks like wet sand. Add the vodka and then the ice water, a tablespoon at a time, and pulse until the dough comes together in large clumps. Gather the dough into a ball and divide in half. Flatten each half into a disk, wrap tightly in plastic wrap, and chill for 30 to 60 minutes.

TO MAKE THE FILLING, combine the apple slices, ⅔ cup hard cider, the brown sugar, granulated sugar, cinnamon, nutmeg, and salt in a large saucepot. Bring to a boil over high heat and cook, stirring often, until the sugar has dissolved and the apples are thickly coated, about 5 minutes.

Meanwhile, combine the remaining 2 tablespoons hard cider with the cornstarch in a small bowl and whisk until smooth. Add the cornstarch mixture to the apples and boil for 1 to 2 minutes, or until the liquid is thick and clear. Remove from the heat, stir in the lemon zest, and allow the mixture to cool for 30 minutes.

Remove both halves of the pie dough from the refrigerator. On a clean, well-floured work surface, roll one disk of the dough into a 12-inch circle. Transfer it to a 9-inch pie plate. Pour the apple mixture into the crust.

¼ teaspoon ground
 nutmeg
¼ teaspoon salt
3 tablespoons cornstarch
Zest of 1 lemon

Roll the second half of the dough into a 12-inch circle and transfer it to the top of the pie. Pinch the edges of the top and bottom crusts together. Trim any excess dough, leaving ½-inch overhang. Crimp the edges decoratively with a fork and cut three 2-inch vents in the center of the top crust. Transfer the pie to the freezer and chill for 1 hour, or until it is very cold and the crust is firm to the touch.

Preheat the oven to 425°F and arrange a rack in the lower third. Brush the top of the pie with the heavy cream and sprinkle with the raw sugar, if using. Bake the pie 20 minutes. Then reduce the oven temperature to 375°F and continue to bake another 40 minutes, or until the crust is golden and the filling is bubbling. (If the edges of the pie brown too quickly, tent them with aluminum foil.)

Cool the pie on a wire rack before serving.

SHAKE IT UP: Substitute beer or lambic (Belgian raspberry beer) for the hard cider.

Cherry Pie with Scotch and Walnut Crumble

ON MY TWENTY-SECOND BIRTHDAY, A FRIEND OF MINE *bought me a glass of scotch at a bar. It was the first time I'd ever tasted the stiff stuff, and I could barely get it down. In fact, it took me the entire night to finish that one drink! Scotch is bracingly strong. For an easy-drinking cocktail, it's best to blend it with sweet, fruity ingredients, such as cherries and lemons. Like someone who's had a bit too much to drink, this pie can be a bit "wobbly kneed," and you may not be able to cut perfect slices. No one I've served it to has ever complained.*

FOR THE CRUST:

1½ cups all-purpose flour

1 tablespoon sugar

¼ teaspoon salt

¼ pound (1 stick) unsalted butter, well chilled and cut into ½-inch cubes

1 tablespoon scotch whiskey

2 to 4 tablespoons ice water

FOR THE CHERRY FILLING:

3 (12-ounce) bags frozen sweet cherries

½ cup granulated sugar

3 tablespoons tapioca flour

2 tablespoons cornstarch

¼ teaspoon salt

3 tablespoons scotch whiskey

Freshly grated zest of a large lemon

FOR THE WALNUT CRUMBLE:

½ cup all-purpose flour

¾ cup chopped walnuts

1 cup old-fashioned rolled oats

⅓ cup granulated sugar

TO MAKE THE CRUST, combine the flour, sugar, and salt in the work bowl of a food processor and pulse to combine. Add the cubes of butter, a few at a time, and pulse until the mixture looks like wet sand. Add the scotch and then the ice water, 1 tablespoon at a time, and pulse until the dough comes together in large clumps. Gather the dough into a ball and flatten into a disk. Wrap tightly in plastic wrap and chill for at least 1 hour.

Roll the dough out on a floured work surface into a 12-inch circle. Transfer to a 9-inch pie plate and crimp the edges with a fork. Transfer the crust to the freezer and chill for 30 minutes.

Preheat the oven to 425°F and adjust the rack to the bottom third.

TO MAKE THE FILLING, gently toss together the cherries, sugar, tapioca flour, cornstarch, salt, scotch, and lemon zest in a large bowl. Let stand for 10 minutes.

TO MAKE THE WALNUT CRUMBLE, combine the flour, chopped walnuts, oats, sugar, brown sugar, cinnamon, and salt in a medium bowl. Add the butter and rub the mixture with clean fingers until it forms moist clumps.

Remove the piecrust from the freezer and fill it with the cherry mixture. Sprinkle the crumb topping over the filling. Bake the pie for 15 minutes. Then reduce the oven temperature to 400°F and continue to bake another 20 to 30 minutes, or until the topping is

¼ cup packed dark
  brown sugar

1 teaspoon ground
  cinnamon

¼ teaspoon salt

6 tablespoons (¾ stick)
  unsalted butter, chilled
  and cut into ½-inch cubes

golden and the fruit is bubbling (if the edges of the crust are browning too quickly, tent them with aluminum foil). Cool the pie on a wire rack for at least 1 hour before serving.

SHAKE IT UP: Substitute bourbon for the scotch.

Cherry Swizzle

2 ounces scotch whiskey

1 ounce freshly squeezed lemon juice

1½ teaspoons superfine sugar

Dash of bitters

Club soda

Cherry, for garnish

Combine the scotch, lemon juice, sugar, and bitters in a cocktail shaker filled with ice. Shake and strain into a glass over ice. Top with club soda, and garnish with the cherry.

MAKES
1
DRINK

Preppy Pink and Green Pie

EVERY AUGUST I GO TO MARTHA'S VINEYARD for vacation. The island gets very crowded in the summer, and at times you can't walk two feet without bumping into someone wearing the preppy, Lily Pulitzer-inspired color combination of carnation pink and lime green. I decided to try to capture the feeling of a New England beach vacation in a pie, which of course wouldn't be complete without a splash of some sort.

FOR THE CRUST:

1½ cups all-purpose flour

1 tablespoon granulated sugar

¼ teaspoon salt

¼ pound (1 stick) unsalted butter, chilled and cut into ½-inch cubes

1 tablespoon vodka or gin

2 to 4 tablespoons ice water

FOR THE FILLING:

1¼ pounds fresh rhubarb, trimmed

1 cup granulated sugar

½ teaspoon cinnamon

½ cup berry liqueur

¼ cup cornstarch

½ cups strawberries, hulled and sliced

FOR THE CRUMB TOPPING:

½ cup all-purpose flour

⅔ cup rolled oats

¼ cup granulated sugar

¼ cup packed light brown sugar

¼ teaspoon cinnamon

¼ teaspoon salt

¾ cup chopped unsalted pistachios

7 tablespoons unsalted butter, diced

TO MAKE THE CRUST, combine the flour, sugar, and salt in a food processor and pulse to combine. Add the butter, and pulse until coarse. Add the ice water, 1 tablespoon at a time, and pulse until the dough comes together in large clumps. Gather the dough into a ball and flatten into a disk. Wrap in plastic wrap and refrigerate for 30 minutes.

On a floured surface, roll the dough to a 12-inch circle. Transfer to a 9-inch pie plate and crimp the edges decoratively with a fork. Put in the freezer while preparing the filling.

TO MAKE THE FILLING, combine the rhubarb, sugar, and cinnamon in a large saucepan. Cook over medium heat until the rhubarb begins to soften and the sugar dissolves, about 5 minutes.

Meanwhile, combine the berry liqueur and cornstarch and stir until smooth. Add to the rhubarb mixture and bring to a boil, stirring constantly until thickened, about 5 minutes. Remove from the heat, transfer to the refrigerator, and cool for 30 minutes.

TO MAKE THE CRUMB TOPPING, combine the flour, oats, sugar, brown sugar, cinnamon, salt, and pistachios in a medium bowl. Cut in the butter until it forms coarse crumbs. Set aside.

Preheat the oven to 375°F and position a rack in the lower third. Remove the crust and the rhubarb mixture from the refrigerator.

Stir the strawberries into the rhubarb mixture, and pour the mixture into the crust. Sprinkle with the crumb topping and bake for 30 to 35 minutes, or until the crust is crisp and golden and the fruit is bubbling.

SHAKE IT UP: Substitute port for the berry liqueur.

Blueberry Rum Pie

MAKES
8
SERVINGS

THIS PIE IS AN ABSOLUTE BREEZE. *The crust is baked very briefly and the filling comes together on the stovetop, making it perfect for hot, humid days when you'd rather be outside than in the kitchen. While fruity drinks are usually made with light rum, such as blueberry mojitos, I found the flavor came through much better in this pie when I used dark rum. Serve with scoops of lemon sorbet or fresh mint ice cream.*

FOR THE CRUST:

1½ cups all-purpose flour

1 tablespoon sugar

¼ teaspoon salt

¼ pound (1 stick) unsalted butter, well chilled and cut into ½-inch cubes

1 tablespoon dark rum

2 to 4 tablespoons ice water

FOR THE BLUEBERRY FILLING:

⅔ cup sugar

3 tablespoons cornstarch

¼ teaspoon ground cinnamon

¼ teaspoon salt

¼ cup dark rum

⅓ cup water

4 cups fresh blueberries, divided

1 tablespoon unsalted butter

TO MAKE THE CRUST, combine the flour, sugar, and salt in the work bowl of a food processor and pulse to combine. Add the cubes of butter, a few at a time, and pulse until the mixture looks like wet sand. Add the rum and then the ice water, 1 tablespoon at a time, and pulse until the dough comes together in large clumps. Gather the dough into a ball and flatten into a disk. Wrap tightly in plastic wrap and chill for at least 30 minutes.

Roll the dough out on a floured work surface into a 12-inch circle. Transfer to a 9-inch pie plate and crimp the edges decoratively. Prick the bottom several times with a fork. Freeze the crust for 30 minutes.

Preheat the oven to 350°F and position a rack in the lower third. Bake the piecrust for 15 to 20 minutes, or until it is pale golden. Remove the crust from the oven and allow it to cool completely.

TO MAKE THE FILLING, combine the sugar, cornstarch, cinnamon, salt, rum, and ⅓ cup of water in a medium saucepan. Stir in 1½ cups of the blueberries and bring the mixture to a boil over medium heat. Boil for a minute or two, until the mixture is very thick and has turned from cloudy to clear. Remove the saucepan from the heat, add the butter, and stir until melted.

Add the remaining 2½ cups of blueberries to the saucepan and stir to combine. Pour the blueberry mixture into the piecrust and refrigerate for about 2 hours, or until set.

SHAKE IT UP: To make a blueberry sangria pie, substitute fruity red wine for the rum.

Spiced Blueberry Mojito

½ ounce freshly
squeezed lime juice

1 teaspoon superfine sugar

5 or 6 fresh mint leaves

8 to 10 fresh blueberries

1 ounce light rum

1 ounce dark rum

Club soda

Lime wedge, for garnish

Combine the lime juice, superfine sugar, mint leaves, and blueberries
in a tall glass. Muddle them until the sugar dissolves. Fill the glass
halfway with ice and add both the rums. Top with club soda
and garnish with the lime wedge.

**Makes
1
drink**

Coconut-Sweet Potato Pie

MAKES 8 SERVINGS

LOTS OF PEOPLE TAKE ADVANTAGE OF THE WINTER HOLIDAYS *and head to the Caribbean for vacation, eschewing itchy wool sweaters, irritating TV specials, and crazy relatives. If you can't escape this year, at least you can bake this pie. The coconut milk provides a taste of the tropics, and the rum will soothe your frazzled nerves.*

FOR THE CRUST:

1½ cups all-purpose flour

1 tablespoon granulated sugar

¼ teaspoon salt

¼ teaspoon baking powder

2 tablespoons shredded unsweetened coconut (optional)

¼ pound (1 stick) unsalted butter, well chilled and cut into ½-inch cubes

1 teaspoon coconut rum

4 to 6 tablespoons ice water

FOR THE FILLING:

2 large sweet potatoes (about 1¾ pounds)

¼ cup packed light brown sugar

⅔ cup canned, unsweetened coconut milk (do not use light coconut milk)

3 tablespoons coconut rum

3 large eggs

½ teaspoon ground cinnamon

¼ teaspoon salt

TO MAKE THE CRUST, combine the flour, sugar, salt, baking powder, and coconut, if using, in the work bowl of a food processor and pulse to combine. Add the cubes of butter and pulse until the mixture looks like wet sand. Add the coconut rum and then the ice water, 1 tablespoon at a time, and pulse until the dough comes together in large clumps. Gather the dough into a ball and flatten into a disk. Wrap tightly in plastic wrap and chill in the refrigerator for 1 hour.

Roll the dough out on a floured work surface into a 12-inch circle. Transfer to a 9-inch pie plate and crimp the edges with a fork. Transfer the crust to the refrigerator and chill while you make the filling.

Preheat the oven to 350°F.

TO MAKE THE FILLING, pierce the potatoes several times with a fork. Bake the potatoes until they are tender and yield easily when pierced with a knife, about 1 hour and 15 minutes. Remove from the oven and cool slightly. Increase the oven temperature to 400°F, and position the rack in the lower third of the oven.

Cut open the potatoes and scrape the flesh into a large bowl. Discard the skins. Mash the potatoes with a fork until very smooth. You should have about 1½ cups.

Whisk the brown sugar, coconut milk, coconut rum, eggs, cinnamon, and salt into the mashed sweet potatoes. Pour the mixture into the chilled crust and bake for about 45 minutes, or until the pie is barely set in the center. Transfer to a wire rack and cool.

SHAKE IT UP: Substitute dark or light rum for the coconut rum. Substitute 1½ cups canned pumpkin purée (not pumpkin pie filling) for the sweet potatoes.

Margarita Meringue Pie

ONE PART LEMON MERINGUE, *one part key lime, and one part margarita, this tequila-spiked pie is incredibly refreshing and perfect for backyard summer cookouts. As meringue pies can sometimes "bleed" at the edges, it's best to keep it chilled until just before serving. Unfortunately, that means you can't take it with you to the beach!*

FOR THE CRUST:

1½ cups all-purpose flour

1 tablespoon sugar

¼ teaspoon salt

¼ pound (1 stick) unsalted butter, chilled and cut into ½-inch cubes

1 tablespoon tequila

2 to 4 tablespoons ice water

FOR THE LIME FILLING:

1¼ cups sugar

1¼ cups water

5 tablespoons cornstarch

5 large egg yolks

2 tablespoons tequila

¼ teaspoon salt

½ cup freshly squeezed lime juice (from about 3 limes)

Zest of 1 lime

2 tablespoons freshly squeezed orange juice

Zest of 1 small orange

2 tablespoons unsalted butter

(continued on next page)

TO MAKE THE CRUST, combine the flour, sugar, and salt in the work bowl of a food processor and pulse to combine. Add the cubes of butter, and pulse until the mixture looks like wet sand. Add the tequila and then add the ice water, 1 tablespoon at a time, and pulse until the dough comes together in large clumps. Gather the dough into a ball and flatten into a disk. Wrap tightly in plastic wrap and chill in the refrigerator for 30 minutes.

Roll the dough out on a floured work surface into a 12-inch circle. Transfer it to a 9-inch pie plate and crimp the edges decoratively with a fork. Prick the bottom of the crust a few times with a fork. Transfer the crust to the freezer and chill for 30 minutes.

Preheat the oven to 350°F and position a rack in the lower third. Bake the crust until it is pale golden, about 15 minutes. Remove the crust from oven and allow it to cool completely on a wire rack.

TO MAKE THE LIME FILLING, whisk 1¼ cups sugar, 1¼ cups water, 5 tablespoons cornstarch, egg yolks, tequila, and salt in a medium saucepan. Cook over medium heat, whisking constantly, until the mixture comes to a boil. Continue to cook 2 to 3 minutes, or until the mixture thickens. Remove from the heat and stir in the lime juice, lime zest, orange juice, orange zest, and butter, and whisk until smooth. Allow the filling to cool completely, and then pour it into the piecrust and refrigerate for at least 2 hours or overnight.

(continued on next page)

FOR THE MERINGUE:

1/3 cup sugar

1 tablespoon cornstarch

5 large egg whites

1/2 teaspoon cream
of tartar

TO MAKE THE MERINGUE, preheat the oven to 350°F. In a small bowl, mix 1/3 cup sugar with 1 tablespoon cornstarch. In a large bowl, beat the egg whites until frothy. Add the cream of tartar and beat until the egg whites hold soft peaks. Add the sugar mixture, one tablespoon at a time, beating constantly. Beat until stiff peaks form.

Spoon dollops of meringue over the chilled pie, covering the filling completely. Bake the pie until the meringue is lightly toasted, about 12 minutes. Transfer to a rack to cool. Chill the pie for 1 hour in the refrigerator before serving.

Beer Margaritas

4 (12-ounce) light-flavored beers,
such as Tecate or Corona

1 cup tequila

1/2 cup orange liqueur, such as Grand Marnier

1 cup frozen limeade concentrate, thawed

Lime wedges

Kosher salt

**MAKES
6 TO 8
DRINKS**

Combine the beer, tequila, orange liqueur, and limeade in a large pitcher and stir to blend. Rub the rim of each glass with a lime wedge and dip the glasses in the salt. Fill the glasses with ice and divide the beer margaritas among them.

Cranberry, Chocolate, and Pecan Pie

AT HOLIDAY MEALS, PECAN PIE always seems to be the last dessert to go—everyone gravitates to the apple and pumpkin pies first. I think it's because some pecan pies can be dense, heavy, and taste a bit monotonous. I guarantee this isn't one of them! The cranberries, chocolate, and bourbon add contrasting tart, rich, and smoky flavors. There won't be a single leftover slice.

FOR THE CRUST:

1½ cups all-purpose flour

1 tablespoon sugar

¼ teaspoon salt

¼ pound (1 stick) unsalted butter, well chilled and cut into ½-inch cubes

1 tablespoon bourbon

2 to 4 tablespoons ice water

FOR THE FILLING:

1½ cups fresh cranberries

1 cup sugar

¼ cup bourbon

1 cup light corn syrup

2 tablespoons butter

2 ounces unsweetened chocolate

3 large eggs

TO MAKE THE CRUST, combine the flour, sugar, and salt in the work bowl of a food processor and pulse to combine. Add the cubes of butter, a few at a time, and pulse until the mixture looks like wet sand. Add the bourbon and then add the ice water, 1 tablespoon at a time, and pulse until the dough comes together in large clumps. Gather the dough into a ball and flatten into a disk. Wrap tightly in plastic wrap and chill for at least 30 minutes.

Roll the dough out on a floured work surface into a 12-inch circle. Transfer to a 9-inch pie plate and crimp the edges decoratively with a fork. Chill the crust in the refrigerator while you make the filling.

Arrange a rack in the lower third of the oven and preheat the oven to 350°F.

TO MAKE THE FILLING, combine the cranberries, sugar, bourbon, and corn syrup in a medium saucepan. Bring to a simmer and cook until the cranberries soften and the mixture thickens, 6 to 8 minutes. Add the butter and chocolate and stir until melted. Remove the saucepan from the heat and allow the mixture to cool for 10 to 15 minutes, or until just warm.

In a small bowl, whisk the eggs until frothy and well blended. Add the eggs to the cooled cranberry mixture, and stir to combine.

Remove the piecrust from the refrigerator and arrange the pecan halves over the bottom. Pour the cranberry filling over the pecans. Bake until the filling is slightly puffed and barely set, about 45 minutes. Cool the pie completely on a wire rack.

SHAKE IT UP: Substitute scotch or whiskey for the bourbon.

Irish Cream Pie

IN THE 1970S, THE *NEW YORK TIMES published a recipe for a brandy Alexander cream pie. A man named Dick Taeuber read the article, took the idea, and ran. He devised more than fifty boozy variations (using a basic ratio of 3 eggs to ½ cup booze to 1 cup of heavy cream) and gave them wacky names like the Pink Squirrel and the Midnight Cowboy. I streamlined my version by using only one type of booze. This recipe is a must for Saint Patrick's Day.*

FOR THE CRUST:

32 chocolate wafer cookies, such as Nabisco, slightly crushed

4 tablespoons unsalted butter, melted

¼ teaspoon salt

FOR THE IRISH CREAM FILLING:

½ cup water

1 (0.25-ounce) envelope unflavored gelatin

⅔ cup sugar, divided

¼ teaspoon salt

3 large eggs, separated

½ cup Irish cream liqueur, such as Bailey's

FOR THE WHIPPED CREAM TOPPING:

1 cup heavy cream

1 tablespoon sugar

Preheat the oven to 350°F.

TO MAKE THE CRUST, pulse the chocolate cookies in a food processor until finely ground (you should have about 1½ cups). Add the melted butter and salt and pulse until the crumbs are moistened. Press the crumbs into the bottom and up the sides of a 9-inch pie plate. Bake the crust until set, about 10 minutes. Cool completely on a wire rack.

TO MAKE THE IRISH CREAM FILLING, put the water in a medium saucepan and sprinkle the gelatin over it. Allow it to soften for 5 minutes, and then stir in ⅓ cup of the sugar, the salt, and the egg yolks. Cook over low heat, stirring constantly until the mixture thickens. Do not boil. Remove the saucepan from the heat and stir in the Irish cream liqueur. Transfer the mixture to a large bowl and refrigerate 20 to 30 minutes, or until the mixture mounds slightly and is just beginning to set.

Meanwhile, in a large bowl beat the egg whites with an electric mixer until foamy. Add the remaining ⅓ cup sugar and beat until stiff peaks form. Carefully fold the egg white mixture into the Irish cream liqueur mixture until just incorporated.

TO MAKE THE WHIPPED CREAM TOPPING, beat the cream in a large bowl with an electric mixer until it holds soft peaks. Carefully fold the whipped cream into the Irish cream liqueur mixture. Pour the filling into the cooled piecrust and chill for at least 4 hours and up to overnight before serving.

SHAKE IT UP: Substitute Kahlùa for the Irish cream liqueur, and coffee for the water.

Strawberry-Port Linzertorte

MAKES
8
SERVINGS

SEVERAL TIMES A MONTH, KEVIN CRAWLEY LEADS *cooking classes at his restaurant, Coriander Bistro, in Sharon, Massachusetts. The classes are done demonstration style (he prepares the recipes while the audience eats them), and attending one makes you feel like you've somehow crossed over and are now actually living inside the Food Network. One of Kevin's best recipes is for a nutty raspberry linzertorte. I've adapted it here, using strawberries and ruby port. This is my mother's favorite dessert to serve when entertaining.*

FOR THE DOUGH:

1½ cups slivered almonds

⅔ cup sugar, divided

2 cups all-purpose flour

1 teaspoon ground cinnamon

½ teaspoon baking powder

¼ teaspoon salt

¼ pound (1 stick) unsalted
  butter, softened

¼ cup shortening

3 large egg yolks

FOR THE FILLING:

1½ cups strawberry
  preserves

3 tablespoons ruby port

TO MAKE THE DOUGH, combine the almonds and ⅓ cup of the sugar in a food processor and pulse until coarse. Add the remaining ⅓ cup sugar, the flour, cinnamon, baking powder, and salt and pulse to combine. Add the butter, shortening, and the egg yolks and pulse until the dough begins to come together in a ball. Turn the dough out and divide into two pieces, one slightly bigger than the other. Flatten each piece into a disk, wrap in plastic, and refrigerate for 30 minutes.

TO MAKE THE FILLING, combine the strawberry preserves and the port in a small bowl and stir until well combined.

Preheat the oven to 350°F and position a rack in the bottom third. Roll the larger piece of dough out on a floured work surface to a 12-inch circle. Transfer to a 9-inch tart pan with a removable bottom and press up the sides.

Roll the second piece of dough to a 12-inch circle. Cut into strips. Transfer the strips to a baking sheet and freeze for 15 minutes.

Pour the strawberry mixture into the tart shell and smooth the surface. Remove the dough strips from the freezer and arrange half horizontally and half vertically across the tart, creating a lattice pattern.

Bake the tart until the crust is golden brown and the filling is bubbling, about 40 minutes. Cool completely on a wire rack. Remove the outer ring of the tart pan, cut into wedges and serve.

SHAKE IT UP: Substitute raspberry liqueur, such as framboise, or fruity red wine for the port.

Nightcap Tart

MAKES 10 TO 12 SERVINGS

WHEN I WAS GROWING UP, I THOUGHT a "nightcap" was a cappuccino you drank before bed. Of course, I've since learned that it's an alcoholic drink—and that a person invited up for one rarely does any actual sleeping. This tart is my attempt to marry both versions of a nightcap (one coffee, one booze) in a dessert. It's deep, dark, and truly decadent.

FOR THE CRUST:

32 chocolate wafer cookies, such as Nabisco, slightly crushed

4 tablespoons (½ stick) unsalted butter, melted

¼ teaspoon salt

FOR THE FILLING:

12 ounces bittersweet or semisweet chocolate, chopped

¾ cup heavy cream

2 tablespoons sugar

2 large eggs

¼ cup coffee liqueur, such as Kahlùa

Preheat the oven to 350°F.

TO MAKE THE CRUST, pulse the chocolate cookies in a food processor until finely ground (you should have about 1½ cups). Add the melted butter and the salt, and pulse until the crumbs are moistened. Press the crumbs into the bottom and up the sides of a 9-inch tart pan with a removable bottom. Place the tart pan on a cookie sheet and set aside.

TO MAKE THE FILLING, place the chopped chocolate in a large bowl. In a small saucepan, heat the heavy cream over low heat until it is steaming and there are tiny bubbles at the edge of the pan (do not boil). Pour the hot cream over the chocolate and stir until the chocolate is melted and smooth. Stir in the sugar.

In a small bowl, whisk the eggs together with the coffee liqueur. Gradually add the egg mixture to the chocolate mixture and whisk until smooth. Pour the filling into the tart crust.

Bake the tart until the edges are puffed and the center is barely set, about 30 minutes. Transfer to a wire rack to cool completely, and then store in the refrigerator. Bring the tart to room temperature before serving.

SHAKE IT UP: Substitute Irish cream liqueur for the coffee liqueur.

Nightcap

1 ounce coffee liqueur, such as Kahlùa
½ ounce brandy
1 ounce cream
Hot coffee (regular or decaf)
Chocolate shavings, for garnish (optional)

Combine the coffee liqueur, brandy, and cream in a mug.
Add the hot coffee and stir to combine.
Sprinkle with the chocolate shavings, if using.

**MAKES
1
DRINK**

Grasshopper Tart
with Chocolate Chips

**MAKES
8 TO 10
SERVINGS**

DESSERTS DON'T GET MUCH MORE RETRO *than grasshopper pie. It was a 1960s dinner party staple, right up there with Rumaki and pigs-in-blankets. I've added chocolate chips to this version. I think they give the tart an interesting, almost chunky texture, like mint-chip ice cream. Make a pitcher of Double Mint Fizzes and invite some friends over for dessert and a "Mad Men" marathon.*

FOR THE CRUST:

32 chocolate wafer cookies, such as Nabisco, coarsely crushed

5 tablespoons unsalted butter, melted and cooled

FOR THE FILLING:

3 large egg yolks

⅓ cup sugar

¼ teaspoon salt

1¾ cups heavy cream, divided

2½ teaspoons unflavored gelatin

¼ cup crème de menthe

2 tablespoons crème de cacao

2 drops green food coloring (optional)

½ cup miniature semisweet chocolate chips

Preheat the oven to 350°F.

TO MAKE THE CRUST, place the chocolate wafer cookies in the work bowl of a food processor and process to fine crumbs. Add the melted butter and pulse to blend.

Press the crumb mixture into the bottom and up the sides of an 11-inch tart pan with a removable bottom. Bake the crust until it looks set, about 10 minutes. Remove the crust from the oven and allow it to cool completely.

TO MAKE THE FILLING, whisk the egg yolks, sugar, and salt together in a medium bowl until thickened and pale yellow. Set aside.

Pour ½ cup of the cream into a small saucepan. Sprinkle with the gelatin. Let stand for 5 minutes to soften, and then cook over low heat for about 2 minutes, or until almost simmering (you will see steam rising from the surface of the milk and small bubbles forming at the edge of the pan). Remove from the heat.

Very slowly whisk a few tablespoons of the hot cream into the egg yolk mixture to temper it, and then whisk the yolk mixture back into the saucepan with the rest of the cream. Cook over low heat, stirring constantly, 3 to 5 minutes, or until the mixture is thick enough to coat the back of a wooden spoon.

Remove from the heat and stir in the crème de menthe, crème de cacao, and green food coloring, if using. Transfer the mixture to a large bowl and refrigerate for 20 to 30 minutes, stirring occasionally, until very thick but not quite set.

(continued on next page)

In a large bowl, whip the remaining 1¼ cups of cream with an electric mixer until soft peaks form. Stir 1 cup of the whipped cream into the mint mixture to lighten it. Stir in the chocolate chips, and then fold in the remaining whipped cream. Spread the mixture into the cooled tart crust. Refrigerate the tart until chilled and set, about 6 hours.

Double Mint Fizz

MAKES 1 DRINK

2 ounces gin

1 ounce freshly squeezed lime juice

½ ounce crème de menthe

1 teaspoon superfine sugar

Club soda

Mint sprig, for garnish

Combine the gin, lime juice, crème de menthe, and sugar in a cocktail shaker filled with ice. Shake and strain into a tall glass filled with ice. Top with club soda, and garnish with the mint.

Red Wine Caramel Tart

MAKES 10 TO 12 SERVINGS

RAISE YOUR HAND IF, FOR A LONG TIME, *you thought all caramel came from the supermarket wrapped up in little squares of cellophane. I sure did. But homemade caramel is actually quite simple, and the gooey, buttery results are far superior to anything you can buy at the store. The half-cup measure of wine in this recipe is a minimum. You can reduce any amount of wine to two tablespoons. If you have a whole cup left in a bottle, by all means use it. The flavors will be that much more concentrated.*

FOR THE CRUST:

1¼ cups all-purpose flour

3 tablespoons sugar

¼ teaspoon salt

¼ pound (1 stick) unsalted butter, chilled and cut into ½-inch chunks

1 large egg yolk

1 tablespoon milk

FOR THE CARAMEL FILLING:

½ cup red wine

1½ cups sugar

3 tablespoons corn syrup

¼ teaspoon salt

6 tablespoons heavy cream

6 tablespoons unsalted butter, diced

TO MAKE THE CRUST, combine the flour, sugar, and salt in a food processor and pulse to combine. Add the butter and pulse until coarse. Add the egg yolk and the milk, and pulse until mixture comes together in large clumps. Gather the dough into a ball and flatten into a disk. Wrap in plastic wrap and refrigerate for 30 minutes.

Roll the dough out on a lightly floured work surface into a 12-inch circle. Press into a 9-inch tart pan with a removable bottom. Fold in any excess dough to make a thick edge. Prick the bottom of the crust with a fork. Refrigerate for 30 minutes. Arrange rack in the bottom third of the oven and preheat the oven to 375°F. Bake the crust until it is golden brown, about 20 minutes. (Check the crust after 10 minutes. If it is bubbling up, gently press back into place.) Cool the crust completely on a wire rack.

TO MAKE THE CARAMEL FILLING, pour the wine into a small saucepan and bring to a boil over medium heat. Lower the heat and simmer until the wine is syrupy and reduced to about 2 tablespoons, about 15 minutes. Remove the saucepan from the heat and set aside. In a medium saucepan, combine the sugar, corn syrup, salt, and 6 tablespoons of water. Stir over low heat until the sugar dissolves, then increase the heat and boil until it turns a deep amber color and a candy thermometer registers just shy of 340°F. (Pull the pan off the heat at around 320°F to make sure the caramel doesn't burn.) Remove the pan from the heat and whisk in the cream, butter, and wine.

Pour the caramel into the cooled tart shell. Let the tart cool slightly; then refrigerate for at least four hours before serving.

Plum and Hazelnut Tart

I ADORE PLUMS, SO THIS TART, *which combines both plum jam and fresh plums, is one of my absolute favorites. When I was testing the recipe, I took one over to my boyfriend's apartment. He ate the entire thing! The toasted flavor of hazelnuts is the perfect complement to the sweet fruit. You can't go wrong if you serve each slice warm, with vanilla ice cream.*

FOR THE CRUST:

- ¾ cup hazelnuts, toasted, skinned, and cooled
- 1¼ cups all-purpose flour
- ¼ cup sugar
- ¼ teaspoon salt
- ¼ pound (1 stick) cold unsalted butter, diced
- 1 large egg yolk
- 1 teaspoon pure vanilla extract

FOR THE FILLING:

- 1 cup plum jam
- 3 tablespoons hazelnut liqueur, such as Frangelico
- 2 ripe plums, pitted and cut into bite-size chunks

TO MAKE THE CRUST, pulse the hazelnuts a few times in the work bowl of a food processor until coarsely chopped. Measure out ¼ cup and set aside. Add the flour, sugar, and salt to the remaining hazelnuts, and pulse until the hazelnuts are finely ground. Add the butter a few pieces at a time and pulse until the mixture resembles wet sand. Measure out ½ cup of the flour mixture and mix it with the reserved hazelnuts. Add the egg yolk and vanilla to the remaining flour mixture and pulse until the mixture starts to clump together.

Transfer the dough to a 9-inch tart pan with a removable bottom, pressing gently into the bottom and up the sides. Freeze the crust for 15 minutes.

Preheat the oven to 350°F.

Bake the tart crust in the middle of the oven for 15 to 20 minutes, or until the edges are pale golden.

TO MAKE THE FILLING, combine the plum jam and hazelnut liqueur in a medium bowl. Stir to blend. Add the plums and toss to coat.

Remove the tart shell from the oven and spread the plum mixture over the bottom. Sprinkle the top with the reserved hazelnut-flour mixture. Return the tart to the oven and bake for 15 minutes more, or until the topping is golden and the fruit is bubbling. Cool completely on a wire rack, and then remove the sides of the pan, cut the tart into wedges, and serve.

SHAKE IT UP: Substitute peach jam for the plum jam, two small peaches for the plums, and peach brandy for the hazelnut liqueur.

Rustic Fig Galette

IN ELEMENTARY SCHOOL, *I had a pink Cabbage Patch Kids lunchbox. On the best of days, it was filled with a bologna and cheese sandwich (sans crusts), a small bag of Cape Cod potato chips, a Capri Sun juice pack, and two Fig Newtons. I haven't had bologna in years, but I still love figs: green, black, dried, and fresh. This rustic, homey galette is bursting with the delicate juicy fresh fruits. And I've traded the Capri Sun for sophisticated Sauternes, a sweet French dessert wine.*

FOR THE CRUST:

1¼ cups all-purpose flour

¼ cup fine yellow cornmeal

¼ cup plus 1 tablespoon sugar, divided

¼ teaspoon salt

¼ pound (1 stick) unsalted butter, diced into ½-inch pieces and chilled

2 to 4 tablespoons ice water

FOR THE FILLING:

¼ cup Sauternes

2 pounds ripe fresh figs

TO MAKE THE CRUST, combine the flour, cornmeal, 1 tablespoon of the sugar, and salt in the work bowl of a food processor and pulse to blend. Add the butter, a few pieces at a time, and pulse to blend. Drizzle in the water, one tablespoon at a time, until the mixture comes together in large clumps. Turn out the dough onto a clean work surface. Form it into a ball, flatten it slightly, and wrap it in plastic wrap. Transfer the dough to the refrigerator to chill for 30 minutes.

Roll out the dough on a lightly floured work surface into a 14-inch circle. Carefully transfer the dough to a 9-inch pie plate, leaving at least a 1-inch overhang. Freeze the crust for 30 minutes.

Preheat the oven to 375°F and position a rack in the lower third.

TO MAKE THE FILLING, in a small saucepan, combine the Sauternes and the remaining ¼ cup sugar. Heat over medium heat until it is reduced and syrupy, about 5 to 7 minutes. Remove the saucepan from the heat and allow to cool while you assemble the rest of the galette.

Trim the figs and cut them into ½-inch wedges. Spoon the figs into the crust and pour the cooled Sauternes syrup over them. Fold the edges of the dough up over the figs (it won't cover them completely).

Bake the galette for 35 to 45 minutes, or until the fruit is bubbling and the crust is golden brown. Transfer the baking sheet to a wire rack and allow the galette to cool for 15 minutes.

SHAKE IT UP: Substitute Riesling or another sweet white wine for the Sauternes.

RAiDiNG THE BAR AND THE COOKiE JAR

What is more irresistible than a warm chocolate chip cookie, or a gooey cream cheese brownie? How about a filled-to-the-brim Cosmopolitan made with white cranberry juice, or an icy glass of Dark and Stormy punch made with fresh ginger? Everyone knows that the pairing of cookies and milk is a match made in heaven, but I think cookies and booze are an equally delicious—and far more devilish—combination.

The recipes in this chapter are simple and whimsical. There's not a plain gingersnap or boring shortbread in the bunch. Instead, I've transformed traditional bake sale treats with funky ingredients like poppy seeds, banana chips, and marshmallow cream. While some names may sound familiar (hermits, black and whites), you can rest assured that these aren't your grandmother's snickerdoodles.

Baking cookies is one of my favorite activities on a lazy afternoon. Here are a few helpful hints for success. Know your oven. While best-quality professional ovens heat evenly, most home ovens are a bit uneven. Because of this, it's best to rotate sheets of cookies from top to bottom and from front to back halfway through the baking time. If you are worried about cookies sticking to your baking sheet, use parchment paper. Nothing—not foil, not silicone mats—works better. Sometimes I only want a cookie or two, or I'm afraid if I bake a whole batch I'll eat a whole batch. It's easy to freeze cookie dough. Simply form the dough into balls and freeze them on a baking sheet. Once they're solid, transfer the frozen balls to a zip-top plastic bag. There is no need to thaw them before baking, just pop them in the oven and add an extra minute or two to the baking time. The frozen cookie dough will last up to three months.

As kids, lots of us came home to an after-school snack of Oreos and chocolate milk, or apple juice and oatmeal raisins. Well, think of the cookies and bars in this chapter as the grown-up counterpart to that childhood ritual. What could be better than curling up after work with a platter of hazelnut liqueur-spiked chocolate chunk cookies and a giant glass of wine? Go ahead and dunk. No one is looking.

Chocolate Chunk Cookies
with Nuts and a Nip

EVERY BAKER NEEDS A PERFECT CHOCOLATE CHIP COOKIE *recipe in his or her repertoire, but that doesn't mean they have to be plain or standard. I pulse the hazelnuts in the food processor, which makes the pieces a bit smaller than if chopped by hand. Then I add hazelnut liqueur to ensure that the nutty, boozy flavor infuses every last crumb. Many recipes that call for toasted hazelnuts instruct you to rub every bit of papery skin off the nuts. Who has that kind of patience? Toast the nuts in a 350°F oven for 6 to 10 minutes and then rough them up a bit in a clean kitchen towel. Most of the skin will come off, and don't worry about the rest.*

2 cups all-purpose flour

1 teaspoon baking soda

¾ teaspoon salt

½ pound (2 sticks) unsalted butter, softened

¾ cup packed dark brown sugar

¾ cup sugar

2 large eggs

1 tablespoon hazelnut liqueur, such as Frangelico

2 cups semisweet or bittersweet chocolate chips

1 cup chopped, toasted hazelnuts

Sift the flour, baking soda, and salt together in a medium bowl to combine.

In a large bowl using an electric mixer, beat the butter with the sugars until light and fluffy, about 3 minutes. Add the eggs, one at a time, beating to combine after each addition. Add the hazelnut liqueur and beat to combine.

Gradually add the dry ingredients to the butter mixture and beat just until blended. Stir in the chocolate chips and the hazelnuts. Transfer the dough to the refrigerator and chill for 30 minutes.

Preheat the oven to 375°F.

Drop the cookies by rounded tablespoonfuls onto ungreased baking sheets and bake for 12 to 14 minutes, or until the cookies are golden and set but still a bit soft in the middle. Let the cookies cool on the baking sheets for 5 minutes and then transfer to a wire rack to cool completely.

SHAKE IT UP: Substitute almond liqueur for the hazelnut liqueur and chopped, toasted almonds for the hazelnuts.

"Old-Fashioned" Snickerdoodles

MAKES ABOUT 24 COOKIES

THE OLD-FASHIONED WHISKEY COCKTAIL IS *one of America's first mixed drinks on record, and it's still one of the best. Likewise, the snickerdoodle is one the nation's oldest cookies. According to* Food Lover's Companion *by Sharon Tyler Herbst, it dates back to the early nineteenth century and the name "has no particular meaning or purpose." This recipe combines the classic components of an Old Fashioned—bourbon, bitters, and orange—in a cookie with a cinnamon-dusted surface and soft center.*

2¾ cups plus 2 tablespoons all-purpose flour

2 teaspoons baking powder

¼ teaspoon salt

½ pound (2 sticks) unsalted butter, softened

1½ cups plus 3 tablespoons sugar, divided

2 large eggs

2 tablespoons bourbon

4 or 5 generous dashes bitters

1 tablespoon freshly grated orange zest

1 tablespoon ground cinnamon

Preheat the oven to 375°F. Line two baking sheets with parchment paper.

In a medium bowl, combine the flour, baking powder, and salt.

In a large bowl, beat the butter and 1½ cups of the sugar with an electric mixer until light and fluffy, about 3 minutes. Add the eggs, one at a time, beating well after each addition. Add the bourbon, bitters, and orange zest and beat to combine. Gradually add the flour mixture to the butter mixture and beat until incorporated. (If the dough is very soft, freeze for 10 to 15 minutes before proceeding.)

Combine the remaining 3 tablespoons of sugar with the cinnamon in a shallow bowl. Roll the cookie dough into 1-inch balls. Roll the balls in the sugar-cinnamon mixture and place them on the baking sheets, spacing the balls about 2 inches apart. Using the bottom of a drinking glass, flatten each ball into a disk.

Bake the cookies for 10 to 12 minutes, or until golden brown at the edges but still slightly soft in the middle. Cool the cookies for 5 minutes on the baking sheets, and then transfer to a wire rack to cool completely.

Cinnamon
Old Fashioned

1 (¼-inch thick) orange wheel

1 brandied cherry (or substitute maraschino)

½ ounce simple syrup (page 15)

2 dashes Angostura bitters

2 ounces bourbon

1 ounce club soda

1 cinnamon stick

Muddle the orange wheel, cherry, simple syrup, and bitters
in a cocktail shaker. Fill the shaker with ice and add the bourbon.
Shake and strain into a cocktail glass over ice. Top with the club soda
and garnish with the cinnamon stick.

MAKES
1
DRINK

Double Limoncello Poppy Seed Cookies

MAKES ABOUT 24 COOKIES

AFTER A STICK-TO-YOUR RIBS MEAL, *the idea of a colossal dessert can sometimes be overwhelming. Instead, set out a plate of these delicate cookies along with some fresh fruit and small glasses of limoncello, the sweet-tart lemon liqueur from Italy that is said to aid digestion. They keep well for up to a week, so a batch would make a great hostess gift, too.*

FOR THE COOKIES:

¼ pound (1 stick) unsalted butter, softened

⅔ cup sugar

1 large egg

Freshly grated zest of two large lemons

2 teaspoons limoncello

1⅓ cups all-purpose flour

½ teaspoon baking soda

¼ teaspoon salt

1 tablespoon poppy seeds

FOR THE GLAZE:

1 cup confectioners' sugar

2 tablespoons limoncello

Preheat the oven to 350°F.

TO MAKE THE COOKIES, beat the butter and sugar together in a large bowl with an electric mixer until light and fluffy, about 2 minutes. Add the egg, lemon zest, and 2 teaspoons of limoncello. Beat until combined.

In a medium bowl, sift together the flour, baking soda, and salt. Add half of the flour mixture to the butter mixture and beat until combined. Add the rest of the flour mixture and beat until combined. Add the poppy seeds and beat on low speed just until combined.

Drop heaping teaspoons of the dough onto ungreased cookie sheets, spacing the dough balls about 2 inches apart. Bake the cookies for 12 to 14 minutes, or until they are just beginning to brown at the edges.

Cool the cookies for 5 minutes on the baking sheet, and then remove and cool completely on a wire rack.

TO MAKE THE GLAZE, combine the confectioners' sugar and limoncello in a small bowl. Stir until smooth.

Drizzle the glaze over the cookies and let stand until set, about 15 minutes.

SHAKE IT UP: For lemon-cherry poppy seed cookies, substitute cherry liqueur, such as kirsch, for the limoncello in the glaze. Add a drop of red food coloring, if using. For a gingery twist, substitute ginger liqueur, such as Domaine de Canton, for the limoncello.

Peanut Butter and Port Thumbprints

SWEET, RICH RUBY PORT HAS A JAMMY FLAVOR *that pairs perfectly with peanut butter. Since everyone has an opinion about what makes the perfect peanut butter and jelly sandwich (Smooth or chunky? Strawberry jam, raspberry jam, or grape jelly?), I've left out those specifics. Use whatever you prefer—just don't try to cut off the crusts.*

2 cups all-purpose flour

½ teaspoon baking soda

¾ teaspoon baking powder

¼ teaspoon salt

½ pound (2 sticks) unsalted butter, softened

1½ cups packed light brown sugar

½ cup granulated sugar

2 large eggs

1 teaspoon pure vanilla extract

1 cup peanut butter

1 cup roasted and salted peanuts, coarsely chopped

¾ cup jam or jelly

3 tablespoons ruby port

In a medium bowl, combine the flour, baking soda, baking powder, and salt.

In a large bowl, beat the butter with the brown sugar and granulated sugar until light and fluffy, about 3 minutes. Beat in the eggs, one at a time, and then beat in the vanilla and the peanut butter. Stir in the flour mixture until just combined. Stir in the chopped peanuts. Transfer the dough to the refrigerator to chill for 20 minutes.

Preheat the oven to 350°F. Line two large baking sheets with parchment paper. In a small bowl, combine the jam and the port. Stir until smooth.

Scoop heaping tablespoons of dough and roll them between your palms to form balls. Place the balls on the baking sheet, spacing them 2 to 3 inches apart. Press the center of each ball with your thumb or the back of a small measuring spoon to make a "thumbprint." Carefully fill each cookie with about 1 teaspoon of the jam mixture.

Bake the cookies until they are puffed and slightly browned at the edges, about 15 minutes. Let them cool on the baking sheets for 5 minutes and then transfer them to a wire rack to cool completely.

SHAKE IT UP: Substitute berry liqueur for the port.

Ruby Flip

2 ounces ruby port
½ ounce cream
1 large egg white
1 teaspoon superfine sugar
Freshly grated nutmeg, for garnish

Combine the port, cream, egg white, and superfine sugar in a shaker filled with ice.
Shake vigorously, strain into a cocktail glass, and sprinkle with the nutmeg.

MAKES
1
DRINK

Dirty Girl Scout Cookies

MAKES ABOUT 32 COOKIES

YEARS AGO, WHEN I WAS JUST OUT OF COLLEGE, my friends Jess and Dave hosted a "very grown up" dinner party that quickly took a debacherous turn after someone suggested we make Dirty Girl Scouts, the incredibly sweet—and lethal—cocktail made of equal parts vodka, coffee liqueur, Irish cream liqueur, and crème de menthe. Though I was never a Girl Scout, I've always loved Girl Scout cookies, especially Thin Mints. I thought it would be fun to combine the flavors of the drink and the cookie in one.

FOR THE COOKIES:

½ pound (2 sticks) unsalted butter, softened

1 cup granulated sugar

½ cup packed light brown sugar

2 large eggs

½ teaspoon vanilla extract

2 teaspoons instant espresso powder

2 cups all-purpose flour

⅔ cup unsweetened cocoa powder

1 teaspoon baking soda

1 teaspoon salt

FOR THE GLAZE:

1¼ to 1¾ cups confectioners' sugar

2 tablespoons Irish cream liqueur

1 tablespoon coffee liqueur

1 tablespoon crème de menthe

32 Junior Mint candies

Preheat the oven to 325°F. Line two baking sheets with parchment paper.

TO MAKE THE COOKIES, beat the butter, sugar, and light brown sugar with an electric mixer in a large bowl until fluffy, about 3 minutes. Add the eggs, vanilla, and espresso powder, scrape down the sides of the bowl, and beat to combine.

In a medium bowl, combine the flour, cocoa powder, baking soda, and salt. Gradually beat the dry ingredients into the butter mixture, stopping to scrape down the bowl as needed.

Drop the dough into rounded balls (about 3 tablespoons each) onto the cookie sheets, spacing them 2 inches apart. Bake until the cookies have flattened, about 15 minutes.

Cool on baking sheets for 10 minutes, and then transfer them to a wire rack to cool completely.

TO MAKE THE GLAZE, combine the confectioners' sugar with the liqueurs in a medium bowl and stir with a whisk until smooth. Set the wire rack with the cooled cookies on it over a row of paper towels. Using a spoon, drizzle about 1 teaspoon of glaze over each cookie, and gently press a Junior Mint into the center. Don't worry if the glaze dribbles off the sides of the cookies a bit—it will firm up once it dries.

Dirty Girl Scout

1½ ounces Irish cream liqueur
1 ounce vodka
1 ounce coffee liqueur
1 ounce crème de menthe

Mix together the Irish cream liqueur, the vodka,
and the coffee liqueur. Pour over ice.
Drizzle the crème de menthe on top.

MAKES 1 DRINK

Banana-Chocolate Chip Biscotti

I'M ALWAYS LOOKING FOR AN EXCUSE *to eat cookies for breakfast. Biscotti are perfect for dunking in coffee—and you could even argue that the banana chips count as a serving of fruit! Not convinced? Try them later in the day, dipped in a small glass of Vin Santo (a sweet Italian dessert wine). These biscotti will last for several weeks stored in an airtight container.*

2¼ cups all-purpose flour

2 teaspoons baking powder

¼ teaspoon salt

¼ pound (1 stick) unsalted butter, softened

¾ cup sugar

2 large eggs

3 tablespoons banana liqueur, such as crème de banane

1 cup unsalted banana chips or dried bananas, slightly crushed or coarsely chopped

6 ounces bittersweet or semisweet chocolate, chopped

In a medium bowl, whisk together the flour, baking powder, and salt.

In a large bowl, beat together the butter and sugar until light and fluffy, about 2 minutes. Beat in the eggs one at a time, and then beat in the banana liqueur. Add the flour mixture to the butter mixture in three additions, beating well after each one. Stir in the banana chips and the chopped chocolate with a wooden spoon.

Gather the dough together in a ball and divide in half. Wrap each half in plastic wrap and freeze for 25 minutes.

Preheat the oven to 350°F. Line a baking sheet with parchment paper. Remove the dough from the freezer and, using lightly floured hands, shape each half into a log about 14 inches long and 3 inches wide. Place the logs on the baking sheet and bake for about 30 minutes, or until set. Remove the baking sheet from the oven and reduce the oven to 300°F. Transfer the logs to a wire rack and cool for 20 minutes.

Using a serrated knife, slice each log on the diagonal into ½-inch-thick slices. Place the slices upright on the baking sheet and return the sheet to the oven.

Bake the biscotti until dry to the touch, 25 to 30 minutes. Cool completely on a wire rack. Biscotti will keep for at least two weeks. Store in an airtight container.

SHAKE IT UP: Substitute dark rum or coconut rum for the crème de banane.

Black and White Russian Cookies

MAKES 12 LARGE COOKIES

I ONCE WROTE AN ARTICLE FOR A NEWSPAPER *rounding up the best black and white cookies in Brooklyn. I tasted cookies that were delicate and crispy, cookies that were thick as slices of pound cake, cookies that were slicked with fondant, and cookies that were slathered with buttercream. You might think that after all that, I'd be sick of black and whites. To the contrary—I was inspired to invent my own version. These cookies are a take on the popular white Russian cocktail made from vodka, coffee liqueur, and milk or cream.*

FOR THE COOKIES:

1¼ cups cake flour

1 cup plus 3 tablespoons all-purpose flour

1 tablespoon instant espresso powder

½ teaspoon baking powder

¼ teaspoon salt

¼ pound (1 stick) unsalted butter, softened

¾ cup granulated sugar

2 large eggs

½ cup well-shaken buttermilk

¼ cup coffee liqueur, such as Kahlùa

FOR THE ICING:

2 cups confectioners' sugar

1 tablespoon light corn syrup

1 tablespoon plus 1 teaspoon water, divided

2 tablespoons plus 2 teaspoons coffee liqueur, such as Kahlùa

1 tablespoon unsweetened cocoa powder

Preheat the oven to 350°F. Line two baking sheets with parchment paper.

TO MAKE THE COOKIES, sift together the cake flour, all-purpose flour, instant espresso powder, baking powder, and salt in a medium bowl.

In a large bowl, beat the butter and the sugar with an electric mixer until light and fluffy, about 3 minutes. Add the eggs, one at a time, and beat until incorporated.

Combine the buttermilk and the coffee liqueur in a liquid measuring cup. Gradually add the flour mixture and the buttermilk mixture to the butter mixture in three additions, beginning and ending with the flour, beating just to incorporate after each addition.

Drop six large (about ⅓ cup) spoonfuls of batter onto each baking sheet, spacing them about 3 inches apart. Bake for 15 to 18 minutes, or until the tops of the cookies are puffy and the tops spring back when pressed lightly. Transfer the cookies to a wire rack and allow them to cool completely.

TO MAKE THE ICING, combine the confectioners' sugar, corn syrup, 1 tablespoon of the water, and the coffee liqueur in a medium bowl and stir until smooth. Spoon half of mixture into a smaller bowl and stir in the cocoa powder and the remaining 1 teaspoon of water.

Spread half of the flat "bottom" side of each cookie with the coffee icing and half with the cocoa frosting.

SHAKE IT UP: Substitute Irish cream liqueur, such as Bailey's, for the coffee liqueur.

Pistachio-Coconut Madeleines

MY ORIGINAL PLAN FOR THIS RECIPE *was to make very sophisticated madeleines, which are small shell-shaped French confections on the line between cookies and teacakes flavored with Cognac. But ultimately the Cognac wasn't bold enough to hold its own against the pistachios. The solution? Coconut rum. Coconuts and pistachios aren't the most conventional pairing, but they work exceptionally well together here. You could serve these madeleines with a classic Kir Royal or a tropical Mai Tai.*

A special shell-shaped madeleine pan is needed for this recipe, but don't let that discourage you. They can be found at most cookware and kitchen supply stores for less than ten dollars.

FOR THE MADELEINES:

- ½ cup shelled natural pistachios
- ¼ pound (1 stick) unsalted butter
- ¾ cup all-purpose flour, plus more for dusting pans
- ½ teaspoon salt
- ⅔ cup granulated sugar
- 3 large eggs
- 3 tablespoons coconut rum

FOR THE GLAZE:

- 00 confectioners' sugar
- 3 tablespoons coconut rum

Preheat the oven to 375°F. Grease two madeleine pans with butter, or spray them with nonstick spray. Dust with flour and tap out the excess. Set aside.

TO MAKE THE MADELEINES, pour the pistachios into the work bowl of a food processor and pulse until they are coarsely chopped.

Melt the butter in a small saucepan over low heat and set aside to cool slightly. Combine the flour and salt in a small bowl. In a large bowl, combine the sugar and the eggs. Beat with an electric mixer until light, about 2 minutes. Gradually add the flour mixture and the chopped pistachios and mix until incorporated. Add the melted butter and the coconut rum and mix until smooth.

Carefully spoon 1 heaping tablespoon of batter into each madeleine mold and bake until a toothpick inserted into the center of a madeleine comes out clean, 10 to 12 minutes. Immediately remove the madeleines from the pan and cool on a wire rack.

TO MAKE THE GLAZE, combine the confectioners' sugar and the coconut rum in a small bowl. Stir until smooth. Dip the pretty "shell" side of each madeleine in the glaze and set on a cookie sheet until glaze hardens, about 15 minutes.

SHAKE IT UP: To make chocolate-hazelnut madeleines, omit the pistachios and increase the flour to 1 cup. As a final step before baking, stir ½ cup mini chocolate chips into the batter. Substitute hazelnut liqueur, such as Frangelico, for the coconut rum.

Chocolate Whoopie Pies with
Orange Liqueur Cream

MAKES 8 WHOOPIE PIES

BACK WHEN *SEX AND THE CITY* was still airing new episodes on HBO, I went through a major Cosmopolitan phase. I bought myself a set of fancy martini glasses and all the cocktail ingredients, including a big bottle of Grand Marnier that took me ages to finish. Besides vodka and cranberry juice, what goes with orange liqueur? Chocolate. These whoopie pies have rich, fudgy cakes that perfectly offset the delicate, floral cream filling.

FOR THE CAKES:

1 cup all-purpose flour

1 cup cake flour

½ cup unsweetened cocoa powder

1 teaspoon salt

1 cup milk

1 teaspoon vanilla extract

¼ pound (1 stick) unsalted butter, softened

1 cup packed light brown sugar

1 large egg

FOR THE CREAM FILLING:

¼ pound (1 stick) unsalted butter, softened

1¼ cups confectioners' sugar

1½ cups marshmallow cream

2 tablespoons orange liqueur

Preheat the oven to 350°F. Line two baking sheets with parchment paper or Silpat mats.

TO MAKE THE CAKES, whisk together the flours, cocoa powder, and salt in a medium bowl. In a small bowl, whisk together the milk and vanilla.

In a large bowl, using an electric mixer, beat together the butter and light brown sugar until light and fluffy, about 3 minutes. Add the egg and beat until smooth. With the mixer on low speed, alternately add the flour and buttermilk in three additions, beginning and ending with the flour. Scrape down the sides of the bowl and beat until just combined.

Using a ¼ cup measure, drop mounds of dough onto the prepared cookie sheets, spacing them 2 inches apart. You should have 8 cookies on each sheet. Bake until cookies are puffed and spring back when touched, about 12 minutes. Cool the cookies for 5 minutes on the cookie sheets, and then transfer them to a wire rack to cool completely.

TO MAKE THE CREAM FILLING, beat together the butter, confectioners' sugar, and marshmallow cream in a large bowl using an electric mixer. Add the orange liqueur and beat until smooth.

To assemble the whoopie pies, spread heaping tablespoons of the cream onto the flat side of half the cookies. Top with remaining cookies.

Clearly Cosmo

2 ounces vodka
1 ounce orange liqueur
1 ounce white cranberry juice
½ ounce freshly squeezed lime juice
Thin slice of fresh orange

Combine the vodka, orange liqueur, cranberry juice,
and lime juice in a cocktail shaker. Fill with ice, shake, and then strain
into a martini glass and garnish with the orange slice.

MAKES
1
DRINK

Dark and Stormy Hermits
with Raisins and Rum

WHAT'S A GIRL GOT TO DO TO GET A DECENT HERMIT THESE DAYS? *Make them herself, I guess. Most of the recipes I've come across in recent years for these classic New England bars call for making them like drop cookies, or frosting them with icing. But the hermits I relished as a child were baked in logs and cut into squares, and served with no garnishes except for a glass of milk. My recipe stays true to the hermit's humble roots, but it does include dark rum, which enhances the flavor of the raisins and calls to mind the dark and stormy cocktail made with rum and ginger beer.*

¾ cup raisins

¼ cup dark rum

2 cups all-purpose flour

1½ teaspoons baking soda

1 teaspoon ground cinnamon

½ teaspoon ground ginger

½ teaspoon ground allspice

¼ teaspoon ground cloves

¼ teaspoon salt

¼ pound (1 stick) unsalted butter, softened

¾ cup packed light brown sugar

2 large eggs

¼ cup molasses

In a small bowl, combine the raisins with the rum and let stand for at least 30 minutes, or until the raisins are softened and slightly plump.

Preheat the oven to 350°F. Line a baking sheet with parchment paper and set aside.

In a medium bowl, sift together the flour, baking soda, cinnamon, ginger, allspice, cloves, and salt.

In a large bowl, beat the butter and sugar with an electric mixer until light and fluffy, about 3 minutes. Add the eggs, one at a time, beating well after each addition. Add the molasses and beat until combined, scraping down the sides of the bowl as necessary. Gradually add the flour to the butter mixture and beat until incorporated. Add the raisins and the rum and beat until just incorporated. Transfer the dough to the refrigerator and chill for 30 minutes.

Remove the dough from the refrigerator and turn out onto a lightly floured work surface. Divide the dough in half and shape each half into a log about 12 inches long and 2 inches wide. Transfer the logs to the prepared baking sheet and bake until they are set and golden, about 20 minutes. Cool on a wire rack, and then cut each log crosswise into 9 pieces.

SHAKE IT UP: Substitute whiskey for the rum.

Dark and Stormy Punch

MAKES 6 TO 8 DRINKS

1 tablespoon freshly grated ginger

1 lime, cut crosswise into thin wheels

½ cup freshly squeezed lime juice

¼ cup simple syrup

2 cups dark rum

4 cups ginger beer

In a large pitcher, combine the grated ginger,
lime slices, lime juice, and simple syrup. Stir in the rum and then
the ginger beer. Serve in tall glasses over ice.

Apricot Brandy Bars

MAKES 12 BARS

ONE OF THE BEST JOBS I EVER HAD *was as the recipe tester for* The Veselka Cookbook. *Veselka is a New York institution, one part traditional Ukrainian restaurant and one part all-night diner. I spent months cooking up borscht and pierogis, but my favorite chapter was the one on desserts. Lisa Staub, Veselka's pastry chef, graciously allowed me to adapt her wonderful recipe for Raspberry-Apricot Bars. I streamlined it by omitting the raspberry jam and pumped up the apricot flavor with fruity brandy.*

FOR THE CRUST:

12 tablespoons (1½ sticks) unsalted butter, softened

1 cup sugar

1 teaspoon pure vanilla extract

1 large egg

2¼ cups all-purpose flour

FOR THE FILLING:

1 cup apricot preserves

¼ cup apricot brandy

4 ounces almond paste

4 tablespoons (½ stick) unsalted butter, softened

⅓ cup sugar

⅛ teaspoon salt

1 large egg plus 1 egg yolk

¼ cup all-purpose flour

Grease a 9 x 9-inch baking pan with butter or nonstick spray. Line with parchment and dust with flour, tapping out the excess. Set aside.

TO MAKE THE CRUST, combine the butter and sugar in a large bowl. Beat with an electric mixer until light and fluffy, about 3 minutes. Add the vanilla and the egg and beat until combined. Gradually add the flour and beat until combined. Gather the dough into a ball and wrap in plastic. Refrigerate for 30 minutes.

On a lightly floured work surface roll the dough out into a 12-inch square and transfer to the prepared pan. Press the dough up the sides, prick the bottom, and crimp the edges with a fork. Freeze the crust for 2 hours. Preheat the oven to 350°F. Bake the crust until it is light golden brown, about 20 minutes. Set the crust aside to cool. Leave the oven on at 350°F.

TO MAKE THE FILLING, combine the apricot preserves with the apricot brandy in a small bowl. Stir until smooth.

In a large bowl, using an electric mixer, cream together the almond paste, butter, sugar, and salt. Add the egg and the egg yolk, and beat until combined. Add the flour and beat until combined. If the mixture looks too soft, refrigerate it for 30 minutes.

Spoon the almond mixture into a large zip-top bag. Snip off one corner, and pipe diagonal lines (2 inches apart) onto the cooled crust.

Using a small spoon, fill the empty spaces in the crust with the apricot mixture. Return the pan to the oven and bake just until the almond and jam mixtures are set, about 20 minutes. Remove from the oven and cool con a wire rack. Cut into 12 bars and serve.

Sherried Date Crumble Bars with Almonds and Orange

THERE IS A WINE BAR AROUND THE CORNER *from my apartment in Brooklyn that has a divine sherry on the menu. One night, as I was sipping a glass, I told the owner, Adam Robertson, about this book and asked him what he thought would be a good recipe for sherry. "Anything with dates," he said. His eyes lit up. "And almonds. And orange."*

The sherry flavor improves overnight, so bake these bars the day before you plan to serve them. Substitute figs or dried plums for the dates, or use a combination.

FOR THE DATE FILLING:

¾ pound (about 2¼ cups) pitted dates

½ cup packed dark brown sugar

⅓ cup water

⅓ cup dry sherry

1 heaping teaspoon freshly grated orange zest

FOR THE CRUST AND CRUMBLE:

2 cups all-purpose flour

1 cup slivered almonds

1 cup packed dark brown sugar

¾ teaspoon baking soda

¼ teaspoon salt

10 tablespoons (1 stick plus 2 tablespoons) unsalted butter, cut into ½-inch chunks

TO MAKE THE DATE FILLING, combine the dates, brown sugar, water, and sherry in a medium saucepan. Bring to a boil, and then reduce the heat and simmer until the sugar is dissolved and the dates have softened, 3 to 5 minutes. Remove the saucepan from the heat, add the orange zest, and allow the mixture to cool completely. Pulse the date mixture in the food processor (or in a blender) until it is coarsely puréed. Set the purée aside. Wash and dry the work bowl.

Preheat the oven to 350°F. Grease a 13 x 9-inch baking dish with butter, or spray it with nonstick spray. Dust the dish with flour and tap out the excess.

TO MAKE THE CRUST AND CRUMBLE, combine the flour, almonds, brown sugar, baking soda, and salt in the food processor and process until the almonds are finely ground, 6 or 7 good pulses. Add the butter a few chunks at a time and pulse until the mixture begins to clump together.

Transfer half of the flour mixture to the prepared baking dish and press it down evenly. Spoon the date mixture over the crust and smooth it to the edges (it will be very sticky; don't worry if there are some bald spots—it will spread out as it bakes), and sprinkle it with the remaining flour mixture.

Bake 30 to 35 minutes, or until the crust is golden and firm. Cool completely in the pan on a wire rack, and then cut into bars and serve.

SHAKE IT UP: Substitute brandy for the sherry.

Oak Bars

MAKES 12 BARS

THESE BLONDIES ARE BIG, BOLD, AND BUTTERY. *Richly flavored California chardonnays were popular in the 1980s but fell out of favor as people's tastes evolved toward lighter, crisper varietals such as sauvignon blanc and pinot gris. I'm convinced Chardonnay is poised for a comeback. It pairs especially well with seafood—and with buttery desserts! For the best flavor, make sure you use a Chardonnay that has been aged in oak barrels (as opposed to steel).*

1¼ cups all-purpose flour

1 teaspoon baking powder

¼ teaspoon salt

¼ pound (1 stick) unsalted butter, softened

1 cup packed light brown sugar

1 large egg

¼ cup chardonnay

½ cup chopped, toasted cashews

¾ cup butterscotch chips

Preheat the oven to 350°F. Line an 8-inch square baking pan with parchment paper. Grease the paper and the sides of the pan with butter, or spray them with nonstick spray. Dust with flour and tap out the excess.

In a small bowl, combine the flour, baking powder, and salt. In a large bowl, beat the butter and the brown sugar with an electric mixer until light and fluffy, 2 or 3 minutes. Beat in the egg and the chardonnay. Gradually beat in the flour mixture just until combined. Stir in the nuts and the butterscotch chips.

Pour the batter into the prepared pan and bake for 25 to 30 minutes, or until golden at the edges and just set in the center. Cool the blondies completely in the pan on a wire rack, and then cut into squares.

Raspberry Cheesecake Swirl Brownies

MAKES 16 BROWNIES

WHEN WE WERE KIDS, MY BROTHER AND I *once attempted to bake brownies without any adult supervision. We didn't burn the house down, but we did forget to add the flour until 15 minutes into the baking time. Unwilling to admit defeat, I took the pan out of the oven, dumped the flour over the hot, half-baked brownies, and raked everything around with a fork. "There," I proclaimed. "That should work." My brother wrinkled his nose. "I don't know," he said. "It kinda looks like something the dog would eat."*

Needless to say, I've come a long way since then. These brownies are dense, fudgy, gooey, and totally irresistible. With ingredients like raspberries, cream cheese, chocolate, and booze (oh, yeah—and flour) how could they not be?

FOR THE BROWNIES:

1 cup all-purpose flour

½ teaspoon baking powder

¼ teaspoon salt

¼ pound (1 stick) unsalted butter, diced

4 ounces unsweetened chocolate, chopped

1¼ cups sugar

2 large eggs

1 teaspoon pure vanilla extract

2 tablespoons framboise

FOR THE CREAM CHEESE TOPPING:

6 ounces cream cheese, softened

¼ cup sugar

1 large egg yolk

½ teaspoon pure vanilla extract

FOR THE RASPBERRY TOPPING:

⅔ cup raspberry jam

2 tablespoons framboise

Preheat the oven to 325°F. Grease a 9 x 9-inch baking pan with butter, or spray it with nonstick spray. Dust it with flour and tap out the excess.

TO MAKE THE BROWNIES, whisk the flour, baking powder, and salt in a small bowl.

In a medium, heatproof bowl, combine the butter and the chocolate. Set the bowl over a pan of simmering water and heat, stirring often, until the mixture has melted and is smooth. Set aside to cool for 5 minutes.

Add the sugar to the chocolate mixture and stir until combined. Stir in the eggs and then add the vanilla and framboise. Add the flour mixture and stir until combined. Set aside.

TO MAKE THE CREAM CHEESE TOPPING, beat the cream cheese and sugar with an electric mixer in a medium bowl until smooth. Add the egg yolk and the vanilla, and beat until smooth. Set aside.

TO MAKE THE RASPBERRY TOPPING, stir together the raspberry jam and liquor in a small bowl until smooth.

To assemble the brownies, reserve ¼ cup of the brownie batter. Pour the remaining batter into the prepared pan. Alternately dollop large spoonfuls of the cream cheese mixture and the raspberry mixture on top of the batter and then dollop on the reserved brownie

(continued on next page)

batter. Using a butter knife, cut through the batter to create a swirled pattern.

Bake the brownies for 35 minutes, or until a toothpick inserted into the center comes out with only a few moist crumbs attached. Cool the brownies completely in the pan on a wire rack. Cut into squares and serve.

SHAKE IT UP: Substitute orange liqueur for the framboise and orange marmalade for the raspberry jam.

Cuba Libre Brownies

IN *THE ULTIMATE BROWNIE COOKBOOK, Bruce Weinstein and Mark Scarbrough include a recipe for Cola Brownies that is a riff on traditional Southern Coca Cola Cake. I created a "cola cocktail" version by adding white rum. They are exceptionally moist and springy. The lime frosting adds a sunny note that complements the richness of the chocolate, but the brownies are also quite delicious without frosting.*

FOR THE BROWNIES:

1½ cups all-purpose flour

1 teaspoon baking soda

1 teaspoon salt

10 ounces bittersweet chocolate, chopped

½ pound (2 sticks) unsalted butter, softened

1 cup granulated sugar

3 large eggs

¾ cup carbonated cola

¼ cup white rum

FOR THE FROSTING:

¼ pound (1 stick) unsalted butter, softened

3 tablespoons cocoa powder

⅓ cup white rum

4 cups confectioners' sugar

Freshly grated zest of 2 limes

Position a rack in the bottom third of the oven. Preheat the oven to 350°F. Grease a 13 x 9-inch baking pan with butter, or spray it with nonstick spray. Dust with flour and tap out the excess. Set aside.

TO MAKE THE BROWNIES, combine the flour, baking soda, and salt in a medium bowl.

Place the chocolate in a heatproof bowl set over a pan of gently simmering water. Stir constantly until the chocolate is almost melted. Remove the bowl from the heat and stir until the chocolate is completely melted.

In a large bowl, beat together the butter and sugar with an electric mixer until light and fluffy, about 3 minutes. Add the eggs one at a time, beating well after each addition. Add the melted chocolate and beat until well incorporated, about 2 minutes, scraping down the sides of the bowl as necessary.

With a wooden spoon or a spatula, gently stir the flour mixture into the chocolate mixture just until combined. Gently stir in the cola and the rum and then pour the batter into the prepared pan, smoothing it to the edges.

Bake the brownies until a toothpick inserted in the center comes out clean, about 35 minutes. Cool the brownies in the pan completely.

TO MAKE THE FROSTING, beat the butter, cocoa powder, and rum with an electric mixer in a large bowl until smooth. Slowly add the confectioners' sugar, one cup at a time, beating until incorporated after each addition.

Spread the frosting over the cooled brownies. Sprinkle with the grated lime zest, cut into squares, and serve.

STiCKY, SAUCY, AND SPiKED: SPOON DESSERTS

L **ate one August when I was** in college, my friend Peter and I took the bus to New York to visit my roommate Danielle, who grew up in the city and was at home for the summer. Since Danielle and I were accustomed to living together in a dorm room roughly the size of a toddler's shoebox, the past three months apart had felt like an eternity. A reunion celebration was in order.

After taking the wrong subway (and then the right subway in the wrong direction), Peter and I finally made it to Danielle's apartment, where we drank many glasses of cheap white wine before heading out on the town. Hours later, as we drunkenly stumbled down Amsterdam Avenue, buses weaving in and out from the curb, a fire hydrant gushing into the street, the faintest hint of dawn on the horizon, Danielle suggested that we stop at her favorite 24-hour diner for food.

"They have amazing desserts here," she promised, as we slid into a red vinyl booth. A refrigerated revolving display case filled with layer cakes and cream pies glittered enticingly next to the counter.

We ordered, and when the food came Peter devoured his dish of rice pudding like a runner sitting down to a plate of spaghetti and meatballs after a marathon.

"This is absolutely the most delicious thing I have ever eaten in my entire life," he slurred between spoonfuls.

Danielle burst out laughing. "That may be true," she admitted. "But it may also be true that you're just drunk."

I've never been back to that particular diner, so I can't speak to the quality of their rice pudding. However, I do believe wholeheartedly that booze and spoon desserts make a winning combination. The recipes in this chapter are totally bib-worthy: sticky, messy, and gooey. Yet they're also quite impressive, even a tad elegant. Whipped cream, chocolate pudding, and lick-your-fingers fruit sauces never fail to elicit child-like "oohs" and "ahhs" from a crowd. But be forewarned: These desserts aren't for kids—they're some of the booziest in the bunch.

Banana-Rum-Raisin Rice Pudding

AFTER A DELICIOUS MEAL IN PARIS, *I ordered a rum-based dessert. To my surprise, the waiter brought over the rum and the dessert separately. After setting the plate and the bottle on the table, he indicated that I should pour as much rum over my piece of cake as I wanted . . . let's just say I had a very lovely—if a bit loopy—stroll home along the winding cobblestone streets!*

I wasn't quite so heavy-handed when developing this recipe, but the rum flavor is still very intense. The secret to perfect rice pudding is to stick close to the kitchen as it cooks—it needs to be stirred almost constantly.

1½ cups water
¾ cup arborio rice
½ teaspoon salt
⅓ cup dark rum
⅔ cup raisins
2¾ cups milk
½ cup heavy cream
½ cup sugar
½ vanilla bean, split lengthwise
½ cup mashed ripe banana (about 1 large)

Bring the water to a boil in a medium-large saucepan. Add the rice and salt, cover, and reduce the heat to low. Cook until the water is absorbed, about 20 minutes.

Meanwhile, combine the rum and the raisins in a small saucepan. Bring to a boil, and then reduce the heat and simmer until the rum is almost absorbed. Remove from the heat and set aside.

Uncover the rice and add the milk, cream, and sugar. Scrape in the seeds from the vanilla bean and toss the bean into the pot as well.

Increase the heat to medium low and cook, stirring frequently, until the mixture is creamy and thick, about 40 minutes. Remove from the heat and immediately stir in the rum and raisins.

Allow the pudding to cool to room temperature, stirring occasionally, about 30 minutes, and then stir in the mashed banana. Refrigerate until chilled, or spoon into bowls and serve warm.

Chocolate Pots de Booze

FOR A LONG TIME, I NEVER MADE BAKED PUDDINGS *or pots de crème because I didn't own a set of ramekins, nor did I want to buy them and thus further clutter my tiny Brooklyn kitchen. Then a friend told me I could just as easily use coffee mugs (make sure they are a ceramic, ovenproof variety). The pots de crème won't come out looking quite as professional, but I actually like the mismatched, carefree style better.*

6 large egg yolks

⅓ cup sugar

2 tablespoons coffee liqueur, such as Kahlùa

2¼ cups heavy cream

¼ cup whiskey

6 ounces bittersweet chocolate, chopped

Position a rack in the lower third of the oven and preheat the oven to 325°F. In a medium bowl, whisk the egg yolks, sugar, and coffee liqueur. Set aside.

In a medium saucepan, heat the heavy cream and the whiskey over medium-low heat until just barely simmering. Remove the saucepan from the heat, add the chocolate, and stir until smooth.

Whisk a few tablespoonfuls (no more than ¼ cup) of the hot cream mixture into the egg yolk mixture to temper it, and then whisk the egg yolk mixture back into the cream mixture. Strain the custard through a fine mesh sieve into a large bowl.

Divide the custard between six 6-ounce ramekins, custard cups, or ovenproof coffee mugs. Cover each with a piece of aluminum foil. Place the cups in a large baking pan or roasting dish and fill with enough hot water to come halfway up the ramekins. Bake for 50 minutes, or until the custards are set but the centers still jiggle slightly. Remove the custards from the water and remove the foil. Transfer to the refrigerator and chill for at least 4 hours before serving.

SHAKE IT UP: Substitute Irish cream liqueur, such as Bailey's, for the coffee liqueur.

Schnappy Butterscotch Pudding
with Pretzel Brittle

MAKES
6
SERVINGS

HOMEMADE BUTTERSCOTCH PUDDING TASTES NOTHING LIKE *the instant mix varieties available in supermarkets. The flavor is deep and intense—layer upon layer of butter and caramel.*

This recipe makes more brittle than you will need to garnish each pudding. But so what? It lasts for several months and makes an amazing housewarming gift.

FOR THE BUTTERSCOTCH PUDDING:

5 tablespoons unsalted butter

1¼ cups packed dark brown sugar

1¼ cups heavy cream

2 cups milk

4 large egg yolks

3 tablespoons cornstarch

¾ teaspoon salt

3 tablespoons butterscotch schnapps

FOR THE PRETZEL BRITTLE:

1 cup granulated sugar

1 cup packed light brown sugar

¼ pound (1 stick) unsalted butter, diced

2 tablespoons light corn syrup

½ cup water

½ teaspoon baking soda

1 cup butterscotch chips

⅔ cup crushed thin pretzel sticks

TO MAKE THE BUTTERSCOTCH PUDDING, combine the butter and the dark brown sugar in a large heavy-bottomed saucepan. Cook over medium heat until the mixture is smooth and bubbling, 4 to 5 minutes.

Meanwhile, in another medium saucepan, warm the heavy cream over low heat. Slowly and carefully pour the warm cream into the brown sugar mixture. Stir over low heat until smooth and combined, about 2 minutes. Remove from heat.

In a medium bowl, whisk the milk, egg yolks, cornstarch, and salt. Whisk ¼ cup of the warm butterscotch mixture into the egg mixture to temper it, and then whisk the egg mixture back into the rest of the butterscotch mixture.

Return the saucepan to low heat and cook, stirring constantly with a whisk, until the mixture has thickened to a pudding-like consistency, about 7 minutes. Remove the saucepan from the heat (if the mixture is very lumpy, strain it through a fine-mesh sieve into a large bowl). Whisk in the butterscotch schnapps. Divide the pudding between six individual ramekins or custard cups. Chill at least 4 hours and preferably overnight before serving.

TO MAKE THE PRETZEL BRITTLE, combine the sugar, light brown sugar, butter, corn syrup, and ½ cup water in a large saucepot and bring to a boil. Cook over medium heat, stirring every so often, for about 20 minutes, or until it has turned a rich golden color, and a candy thermometer registers 300°F.

(continued on next page)

Remove from the heat and stir in the baking soda. The mixture will foam and bubble viciously (don't stress—that's supposed to happen). Once the foaming subsides a bit, pour the mixture onto a baking sheet and spread it out as much as possible with a spatula. Let stand for about 10 minutes, or until the brittle hardens slightly.

Meanwhile, in a small bowl, melt the butterscotch chips in the microwave for 1 minute. Stir and then return the butterscotch to the microwave and heat for 1 minute more, or until smooth. Pour the butterscotch over the brittle, and spread it to the edges with a spatula. Sprinkle the butterscotch with the crushed pretzels and allow the brittle to cool completely, about 1 hour. Break into large shards.

To serve, garnish each pudding with a piece of brittle. (Leftover brittle will keep for up to six weeks stored in an airtight container.)

SHAKE IT UP: Substitute bourbon or scotch for the butterscotch schnapps.

Butterscotch Hot Chocolate

3½ cups milk
½ cup half-and-half
½ pound bittersweet chocolate, chopped
⅓ cup butterscotch schnapps
4 large marshmallows

Combine the milk and half-and-half in a medium saucepan. Heat until almost simmering (you will see steam rising from the surface and small bubbles forming at the edge of the pan). Remove the pan from the heat, add the chocolate, and whisk until dissolved. Add the butterscotch schnapps and divide the mixture among four mugs. Garnish each with a marshmallow or two.

MAKES
4
DRINKS

Vin Santo-Vanilla Panna Cotta
with Apricot Compote

MAKES 6 SERVINGS

PANNA COTTA LITERALLY MEANS "COOKED CREAM" *in Italian. It tastes like a delectable cross between pudding and gelatin, but it looks far more elegant when unmolded on a pretty dessert plate and garnished with a swirl of brightly colored fruit compote. Vin Santo is a sweet dessert wine from Italy. Serve the rest of the bottle in small glasses alongside the panna cotta, with a plate of store-bought biscotti or shortbread cookies.*

FOR THE PANNA COTTA:

3 tablespoons cold water

1 (1-tablespoon) envelope unflavored gelatin

2 cups heavy cream

1 cup milk

½ vanilla bean, split lengthwise

½ cup sugar

2 tablespoons Vin Santo

FOR THE APRICOT COMPOTE:

12 dried apricots (about ⅔ cup)

½ cup boiling water

2 tablespoons Vin Santo

TO MAKE THE PANNA COTTA, pour the cold water into a small bowl and sprinkle the gelatin on top. Allow the mixture to soften for 5 to 10 minutes.

In a medium saucepan, combine the heavy cream, milk, vanilla bean, and sugar. Bring to a simmer over medium-low heat, stirring occasionally. As soon as the mixture simmers, remove it from the heat, add the softened gelatin, and stir until it dissolves. Stir in the Vin Santo.

Divide the cream mixture between six ramekins, dessert cups, or teacups. Refrigerate, uncovered, until set, at least 4 hours. (Panna cottas can be made two days ahead. Once they have set and are chilled, cover with plastic wrap.)

TO MAKE THE APRICOT COMPOTE, combine the apricots and boiling water in a small bowl. Allow to stand until the apricots are softened, 5 or 6 minutes. Transfer the apricot mixture to a blender and add the Vin Santo. Blend until smooth.

To serve, run a thin-bladed knife around the edge of each panna cotta and invert each over a plate. Remove the ramekins, and garnish with a scoop of the compote.

SHAKE IT UP: Substitute almond liqueur, such as amaretto, for the Vin Santo.

Muscat and Melon Mousse

IN MY EARLY TWENTIES, I LIVED IN A TINY *fourth-floor walk-up apartment with my friend Laura. During the insanely hot and humid summer months, she would make an incredibly refreshing—and inebriating—concoction by hollowing out a melon and filling it with a mixture of white wine and ice cream (stick in two straws and serve!).*

This recipe is my rendition of Laura's fantastic dessert. Instead of combining the ingredients in a melon shell, I've whipped everything together into a cooling, not-too-sweet mousse. Gourmet *published a similar recipe in the early 1990s using Midori, a sweet, bright green melon liqueur.*

½ cup Muscat Sec wine

3 envelopes (about 3 tablespoons) unflavored gelatin

1 (6- to 7-pound) cantaloupe or honeydew melon, sliced, seeded, and cut into chunks

½ cup sugar, divided

¼ cup lemon juice, divided

⅔ cup plain yogurt

Pour the Muscat Sec into a small saucepan and sprinkle the gelatin on top. Let it soften for 1 to 2 minutes, and then cook over low heat, stirring constantly, until the gelatin has dissolved. Remove from the heat and allow to cool.

In a blender, purée half the melon with ¼ cup of the sugar and 2 tablespoons of the lemon juice. With the blender running, slowly pour in half of the Muscat mixture. Transfer the melon mixture to a large metal bowl set in a pan of ice water. Repeat with the remaining melon, sugar, lemon juice, and Muscat mixture, and then add the second half of the melon mixture to the metal bowl.

Stir the melon mixture for 3 to 5 minutes, or until it begins to thicken slightly (its texture should be similar to that of maple syrup or raw egg white). Remove the bowl from the ice water and stir in the yogurt.

Pour the mousse into a large glass bowl and refrigerate for 4 hours or overnight.

Sidecar Soufflé

**MAKES
6
SERVINGS**

INVENTED IN THE 1920S, THE SIDECAR *is a sophisticated cocktail made from Cognac or brandy, orange liqueur, and lemon juice, and served in a martini glass. I've substituted freshly squeezed orange juice for the lemon juice in this soufflé, which gives it a slightly sweeter flavor. Soufflés must be prepared at the last minute and eaten immediately, so serve this at the sort of small dinner party where everyone is hanging out and helping in the kitchen.*

FOR THE SOUFFLÉ:

2 tablespoons unsalted
butter, melted and cooled

2 tablespoons all purpose
flour

1 tablespoon cornstarch

1/4 teaspoon salt

1 1/3 cups milk

5 large eggs, separated

1/2 cup sugar

3 tablespoons orange liqueur

2 teaspoons freshly grated
orange zest (optional)

1/4 teaspoon cream of tartar

FOR THE SAUCE:

1/2 cup sugar

2 tablespoons cornstarch

1/8 teaspoon salt

1 cup freshly squeezed
orange juice

1/4 orange liqueur

1/4 cup cognac or brandy

Position the oven rack in the lower third of the oven. Preheat the oven to 375°F. Grease an 8-cup soufflé dish with buter.

TO MAKE THE SOUFFLÉ, whisk together the melted butter, the flour, cornstarch, salt, and milk in a small saucepan. Heat over low heat, whisking constantly, until mixture thickens, about 6 minutes Remove from the heat.

In a large bowl, whisk the egg yolks with 1/4 cup sugar, orange liqueur, and orange zest (if using) until thick and smooth.

Very slowly, whisk a ladleful (no more than 1/4 cup) of the hot milk mixture into the egg yolk mixture. Whisk constantly until combined. Very slowly add the rest of the milk mixture to the egg yolks, whisking constantly. Set aside.

In a large bowl beat the egg whites and the cream of tartar with an electric mixer until the mixture forms soft peaks. Add the remaining 1/4 cup of sugar and beat to stiff peaks. Fold one-quarter of the egg whites into the egg yolk mixture to lighten, and then gently fold in the remaining egg whites. Pour the mixture into the prepared soufflé dish and bake for 40 minutes, or until puffy and golden.

About 10 minutes before the soufflé is done, prepare the sauce.

TO MAKE THE SAUCE, combine the sugar, cornstarch, salt, orange juice, orange liqueur, and brandy in a small saucepan. Bring to a boil over medium-low heat, stirring constantly until thick and bubbly. Remove from heat and serve immediately with the soufflé.

Orange Sidecar

2 ounces cognac or brandy
1 ounce orange liqueur, such as Cointreau
½ ounce freshly squeezed lemon juice
½ ounce freshly squeezed orange juice

Combine the cognac or brandy, the orange liqueur,
lemon juice, and orange juice in a cocktail shaker filled with ice.
Shake and strain into a cocktail glass.

MAKES
1
DRINK

Berry Chocolate Mousse

MAKES 6 TO 8 SERVINGS

MY FRIEND DARREN ONCE INVITED ME *over to his apartment for what he said would be a "casual, spur-of-the-moment lunch." When I arrived, he had prepared a feast! A whole roasted fish stuffed with Mediterranean herbs, mashed potatoes with kalamata olives, and chocolate mousse for dessert. He used Julia Child's recipe, which I studied before developing this one. The flavor of the berry liqueur comes through very subtly, but it really enhances the chocolate.*

5 ounces bittersweet chocolate, chopped

2 tablespoons unsalted butter

¼ cup berry liqueur, such as framboise

4 large eggs, separated

¼ cup plus 2 tablespoons sugar, divided

1 cup heavy cream

Blackberries, for serving

Combine the chocolate, butter, and berry liqueur in a heatproof bowl set over a pan of simmering water. Stir until the chocolate has almost completely melted. Remove the bowl from the heat and stir until smooth.

In a large bowl, whisk the egg yolks and ¼ cup of sugar until pale yellow, about 2 minutes. Whisk in the melted chocolate mixture.

In a medium bowl, beat the egg whites with an electric mixer until frothy. Add the remaining 2 tablespoons of sugar and beat until the whites hold soft peaks. Set aside, and wash and dry the beaters.

In another medium bowl, beat the heavy cream with an electric mixer until soft peaks form. Stir half of the egg whites into the chocolate mixture to lighten it, and then carefully fold in the remaining egg whites. Carefully fold in the whipped cream. Refrigerate the mousse until chilled. Spoon into bowls, garnish with blackberries, and serve.

SHAKE IT UP: Substitute almond or hazelnut liqueur for the berry liqueur.

Hazelnut Tiramisu

In her memoir Eat, Pray, Love, *Elizabeth Gilbert writes about going to a soccer match in Rome with some newfound Italian friends. When their team loses, instead of drowning their sorrows at a bar (a common American response to athletic defeat), they head to a pastry shop and gorge themselves on desserts.*

The word tiramisu literally means "pick me up" or "make me happy." Traditionally, it is made with Marsala, a Sicilian sweet wine fortified with brandy. For a new twist, I use hazelnut liqueur and chocolate-hazelnut spread. If only they would sell tiramisu at sports arenas instead of boring old peanuts, my boyfriend might get me to go to more games!

6 ounces mascarpone cheese

¼ cup chocolate hazelnut spread, such as Nutella

1 cup plus 3 tablespoons hazelnut liqueur, such as Frangelico, divided

1 cup heavy cream

1 cup warm brewed espresso or coffee

24 ladyfinger cookies, such as Savoiardi

Chocolate shavings, for garnish

Hazelnuts, toasted and chopped, for garnish

Line a standard 9 x 5-inch loaf pan with plastic wrap, allowing the plastic to extend over the sides.

In a large bowl, beat the mascarpone cheese, chocolate hazelnut spread, and 3 tablespoons of the hazelnut liqueur with an electric mixer just until blended and smooth. Set aside. Wash and dry the beaters.

In another large bowl, beat the heavy cream until soft peaks form. Fold the whipped cream into the mascarpone-chocolate mixture. Set aside.

In a medium bowl, combine the espresso with the remaining 1 cup of hazelnut liqueur. Quickly dip each cookie into the espresso-liqueur mixture to saturate it, and then place it crosswise in the bottom of the prepared pan, creating a single layer. (You might have to squish them a bit to make them fit, but don't worry—it will look lovely in the end.) Cover the cookie layer with one-third of the mascarpone mixture. Repeat with another layer of cookies and another third of the mascarpone mixture, and then a final layer of cookies.

Wrap the tiramisu, still in the loaf pan, in another layer of plastic wrap and refrigerate overnight. Transfer the remaining third of the mascarpone mixture to an airtight container, and refrigerate.

When ready to serve, unwrap the tiramisu and invert it onto a serving plate. Spread the remaining mascarpone mixture over the top. Sprinkle with chocolate shavings and chopped hazelnuts, cut crosswise into slices, and serve.

Donut Bread Pudding with
Tennessee Whiskey Sauce

**MAKES
6
GENEROUS
SERVINGS**

IN ADDITION TO APPLES, SQUASH, AND SPINACH, *my local farmers' market also has a stand that sells freshly made donuts showered in cinnamon sugar. One Saturday morning in late fall, the smell was so enticing—warm cake mingling with the crisp leaves—that I couldn't resist buying not just one, but an entire bagful. Later that day I baked them into an irresistible bread pudding drizzled with smoky Tennessee whiskey and sweet cream.*

It's important to use plain cake donuts in this recipe (as opposed to airier glazed varieties), as they better absorb the custard.

FOR THE
BREAD PUDDING:

- 4 tablespoons (½ stick) unsalted butter, melted
- 8 store-bought plain cake donuts, such as Entenmann's
- ½ cup packed light brown sugar
- ¼ teaspoon ground cinnamon
- ⅛ teaspoon ground nutmeg
- 4 large eggs
- 2¼ cups heavy cream or whole milk
- ¼ cup Tennessee whiskey
- 1 teaspoon pure vanilla extract

FOR THE SAUCE:

- 1½ teaspoons cornstarch
- 2 tablespoons Tennessee whiskey
- ¾ cup heavy cream
- 2 tablespoons granulated sugar
- Whipped cream, store-bought caramel sauce or vanilla ice cream, for garnish (optional)

TO MAKE THE PUDDING, lightly brush a 9-inch square baking pan with a little bit of the melted butter. Cut the doughnuts into 1½ to 2-inch chunks and add them to the pan.

In a large bowl combine the remaining butter, brown sugar, cinnamon, and nutmeg. Add the eggs and whisk until blended. Whisk in the heavy cream, the whiskey, and the vanilla. Pour the egg mixture over the doughnuts. Press down gently with a wooden spoon, making sure to submerge all the pieces. Allow the pudding to stand at room temperature for 1 hour, or cover and refrigerate overnight.

Preheat the oven to 350°F. Cover the pudding with a piece of aluminum foil and bake for 30 minutes. Remove the foil and bake the pudding for an additional 15 minutes, or until the custard is set but soft and the tops of the doughnuts are lightly browned.

TO MAKE THE SAUCE, combine the cornstarch and the whiskey in a small bowl. In a small saucepan, combine the cream and sugar and heat over high heat, whisking constantly, 2 or 3 minutes, or until small bubbles begin to form. Continue whisking constantly and add the whiskey mixture (it will bubble vigorously). Continue whisking until the sauce is blended and thick.

To serve, scoop the bread pudding into shallow bowls. Spoon the sauce over the pudding and top with whipped cream, caramel sauce, or vanilla ice cream, if using.

SHAKE IT UP: Substitute dark rum for the whiskey.

Pink Elephant Milkshakes

MAKES 4 TO 5 SERVINGS

IF DRINKING ALCOHOL WERE A SPORT (and some might argue that it is), then the pink elephant would be its mascot. The phrase is most often used in reference to someone who is so drunk they've reached the point of hallucination. I've never seen any pink elephants myself, but then, I've never had more than one of these milkshakes at a time. If you don't have an ice cream maker, substitute store-bought strawberry ice cream.

FOR THE ICE CREAM:

1 pint fresh strawberries, hulled and sliced

3 tablespoons tequila

¾ cup plus ⅓ cup sugar, divided

6 large egg yolks

⅛ teaspoon salt

2¼ cups heavy cream

1 cup milk

FOR THE MILKSHAKES:

1 cup milk

½ cup tequila

Fresh strawberries, for garnish

TO MAKE THE ICE CREAM, place the strawberries in the work bowl of a food processor or blender and pulse a few times until they are coarsely chopped. Transfer them to a bowl and add the tequila and ⅓ cup of the sugar. Cover, and chill in the refrigerator.

In a medium bowl, whisk the egg yolks with the salt and the remaining ¾ cup sugar until they are thick and pale yellow. Set aside.

In a medium saucepan, combine the heavy cream and the milk. Cook over medium-low heat until mixture is barely simmering (you should see steam rising from the surface and small bubbles forming at the edges of the pan). Remove the pan from heat.

Very slowly whisk ¼ cup of the hot cream into the egg mixture to temper it, and then whisk the egg mixture back into the cream mixture. Cook over medium heat for 3 to 6 minutes, or until the mixture thickens and coats the back of a spoon without running.

Remove the saucepan from heat and strain the custard mixture through a fine-mesh sieve into a large bowl. Add the strawberry mixture, cover and chill in the refrigerator at least 4 hours or overnight, and then freeze in an ice cream maker according to the manufacturer's instructions.

TO MAKE THE MILKSHAKES, scoop half of the ice cream into a blender. Add the milk and the tequila, and blend until smooth. Add the rest of the ice cream and blend until smooth. Divide the mixture between four or five large glasses, garnish each with a strawberry, and serve.

SHAKE IT UP: Substitute berry-flavored vodka for the tequila.

Bourbon-Vanilla Ice Cream Sandwich Cookies

MAKES 12 SAND-WICHES

I NEVER MUCH CARED FOR PLAIN OL' SUGAR COOKIES *until I tried a recipe from Cooks' Illustrated that called for brown sugar and browned butter. What a difference! The cookies had an intense, nutty flavor that was completely addictive. I altered the recipe slightly, adapted it to include bourbon, and used it as a base for these boozy ice cream sandwiches. If you don't have an ice cream maker, substitute store-bought vanilla or butter pecan ice cream.*

FOR THE BROWN SUGAR COOKIES:

14 tablespoons (1¾ sticks) unsalted butter, divided

2 cups all-purpose flour

½ teaspoon baking soda

¼ teaspoon baking powder

¼ teaspoon salt

1¾ cups packed dark brown sugar

2 large eggs

1 tablespoon bourbon

½ cup granulated sugar

FOR THE ICE CREAM:

1¾ cups heavy cream

1½ cups milk

1 vanilla bean

7 large egg yolks

¾ cup sugar

¼ teaspoon salt

¼ cup bourbon

TO MAKE THE COOKIES, melt 10 tablespoons of the butter in a small saucepan over medium heat. Cook until the butter is a deep, nutty brown, about 4 minutes. Pour the browned butter into a medium bowl and add the remaining 4 tablespoons of butter. Stir until melted and combined. Set aside to cool slightly.

Meanwhile, whisk together the flour, baking soda, baking powder, and salt in a medium bowl. Set aside.

Add the brown sugar to the cooled butter mixture. Whisk until smooth, and then add the eggs and the bourbon. Stir in the flour mixture. Chill the dough in the refrigerator for 15 minutes.

Preheat the oven to 350°F. Spread the ½ cup sugar on a large plate. Line two baking sheets with parchment paper and set aside. Remove the dough from the refrigerator. Scoop up a ball of dough, about 2 tablespoons, and roll it between your palms to form a ball, and then roll it in the sugar to coat. Place the ball on a cookie sheet and flatten slightly with your fingers or the bottom of a juice glass. Repeat with the remaining dough, spacing balls 2 inches apart on the baking sheets. You should have 12 balls on each sheet, for a total of 24.

Bake the cookies for 12 minutes, or until just set at the edges (don't worry if they look too soft—they will firm up a bit as they cool). Cool the cookies completely on the baking sheets. Then transfer to an airtight container. (Cookies can be made up to three days ahead.)

(continued on next page)

TO MAKE THE ICE CREAM, combine cream and milk in a medium saucepan. Split the vanilla bean in half lengthwise and scrape the seeds into the cream mixture. Drop the vanilla bean into the pan and bring the cream mixture to just under a boil over medium heat. Remove the cream from the heat, cover, and steep for 20 minutes.

Combine the egg yolks with the sugar and salt in a mixing bowl. Whisk until the color lightens. Slowly whisk ¼ cup of the hot cream into the egg mixture to temper it, and then whisk the egg mixture back into the cream mixture. Cook over medium heat for 3 to 6 minutes, or until the mixture thickens and coats the back of a spoon without running. Remove from the heat, strain the mixture through a fine-mesh sieve, and add the bourbon.

Chill the mixture in the refrigerator at least 4 hours, or overnight, and then freeze in an ice cream maker according to the manufacturer's instructions.

To assemble the ice cream sandwiches, place a small scoop of ice cream on the bottom side of one cookie. Top with another cookie and press down slightly to make a sandwich. Repeat with the remaining cookies and the rest of the ice cream. Wrap the sandwiches in plastic wrap and freeze until ready to serve.

Lemon-Cherry Semifreddo
with Pistachios

MAKES
8
SERVINGS

THIS SEMIFREDDO IS A GREAT SUMMER DESSERT OPTION *if you don't own an ice cream maker. Essentially, it's a frozen mousse "loaf," though that doesn't sound quite as appealing as it is in actuality. The bright red cherries and crunchy green pistachios make for a very pretty presentation. Next to the pale semifreddo, the colors are reminiscent of the Italian flag. Serve this after a casual pizza and beer party.*

FOR THE SEMIFREDDO:

⅔ cup chopped toasted pistachios

2 cups heavy cream

¾ cup sugar, divided

8 large egg yolks

½ cup freshly squeezed lemon juice

¼ cup cherry liqueur, such as kirsch

2 tablespoons freshly grated lemon zest

FOR THE SWEET CHERRY SAUCE:

2 cups fresh or frozen pitted sweet cherries

½ cup cherry liqueur, such as kirsch

2 tablespoons sugar

1 tablespoon freshly grated lemon zest

Line a 9 x 5-inch loaf pan with plastic wrap lengthwise and crosswise, leaving an overhang.

TO MAKE THE SEMIFREDDO, sprinkle the pistachios in the bottom of the pan. Set aside.

In a large bowl, whip the cream and ¼ cup sugar with an electric mixer until soft peaks form. Transfer the bowl to the refrigerator and chill. In a medium glass bowl, whisk together the remaining ½ cup sugar, the egg yolks, lemon juice, and cherry liqueur. Set the bowl over a pan of simmering water, whisking constantly, until the mixture is thick and creamy and between 160° and 170°F, 5 or 6 minutes.

Remove the bowl from the heat and place it in a larger bowl filled with ice water to cool. Stir in the lemon zest and allow the mixture to sit for 15 to 20 minutes, or until completely cooled.

Using a rubber spatula, gently fold the whipped cream into the custard mixture until no white streaks remain. Pour the mixture over the pistachios in the loaf pan. Fold the plastic wrap over the top to cover and freeze for at least 8 hours and up to 3 days.

TO MAKE THE SWEET CHERRY SAUCE, combine the cherries, cherry liqueur, sugar, and lemon zest in a small saucepan over medium heat. Simmer, stirring occasionally, until the mixture is warm and the sugar has dissolved. Refrigerate until well chilled.

To serve, unfold the plastic wrap and invert the semifreddo over a plate. Slice the semifreddo crosswise into 1 inch slices and top with a generous spoonful of the cherry sauce.

SHAKE IT UP: For a more intense lemon flavor, substitute limoncello for the cherry liqueur.

Port Ice Cream Sundaes

MAKES ABOUT 1 QUART OR 6 SERVINGS

MY FELLOW SERIOUSEATS.COM FOOD BLOGGER *Adam Kuban once wrote "there's always room for ice cream because it just melts around whatever's already in your stomach." I couldn't agree more. I also think there's always space for a sip or two of port at the end of an evening. Without the food coloring, this ice cream will be only a shade or two darker than vanilla, so if you want a bold wine color, it's best to add it.*

FOR THE ICE CREAM:

1¾ cups heavy cream

1½ cups milk

1 vanilla bean

1 cinnamon stick

6 large egg yolks

¾ cup sugar

¼ teaspoon salt

½ cup port

2 drops red food coloring (optional)

FOR THE CHOCOLATE SAUCE:

1½ cups bittersweet chocolate, chopped

¼ cup milk

¼ cup heavy cream

3 tablespoons port

FOR THE WHIPPED CREAM:

1 cup heavy cream

2 tablespoons sugar

1 tablespoon port

TO MAKE THE ICE CREAM, combine the cream and milk in a heavy, medium saucepan. Split the vanilla bean in half and scrape out the seeds. Add the seeds and the pod to the saucepan along with the cinnamon stick. Bring the mixture to just under a boil over medium heat (bubbles will form at the edge of the pan). Remove the saucepan from the heat, cover, and allow to steep for 15 minutes.

Meanwhile, whisk together the egg yolks, sugar, and salt in a medium bowl until light and creamy. Carefully and slowly whisk a few spoonfuls (no more than ¼ cup) of the hot cream mixture into the yolk mixture to temper it, and then whisk the entire yolk mixture into the saucepan with the cream. Cook over medium heat, stirring constantly, for 3 to 6 minutes, or until the custard thickens enough to coat the back of a wooden spoon.

Remove the saucepan from heat and pour the custard through a fine-mesh sieve into a large bowl. Add the port and stir to combine. Cover the bowl with plastic wrap and refrigerate at least 4 hours, and then freeze in an ice cream maker according to its instructions.

TO MAKE THE CHOCOLATE SAUCE, place the chopped chocolate in a medium bowl. Combine the milk and cream in a small saucepan and heat until barely simmering. Pour the hot cream mixture over the chocolate and stir until smooth. Add the port and stir until combined.

TO MAKE THE WHIPPED CREAM, combine the cream, sugar, and port in a large bowl. Beat with an electric mixer until soft peaks form.

To serve, scoop the ice cream into bowls and top with the chocolate sauce and then the whipped cream.

Beer Profiteroles with Chocolate-Beer Sauce

MAKES 6 SERVINGS

IF THIS RECIPE SEEMS A BIT INTIMIDATING, *crack open a cold one before tackling the first step. The end results—scoops of beer ice cream nestled in pastry puffs and dripping with beer-infused chocolate sauce—are well worth it. If you're short on time, substitute store-bought coffee or vanilla ice cream for homemade. Or, for a dessert Homer Simpson would love, use purchased donut holes in place of the puff pastry. The ice cream can be made up to five days ahead, and the profiteroles will keep well for a day or two stored in an airtight container.*

FOR THE BEER ICE CREAM:

2 1/2 cups heavy cream

1 1/2 cups milk

5 large egg yolks

3/4 cup granulated sugar

1/4 teaspoon salt

1 teaspoon pure vanilla extract

1 cup (8 ounces) chocolate stout, or other dark beer

FOR THE PROFITEROLES:

1/2 cup water

1/4 cup whole milk

6 tablespoons unsalted butter

1/4 teaspoon salt

3/4 cup all-purpose flour

3 large eggs

FOR THE CHOCOLATE-BEER SAUCE:

8 ounces bittersweet chocolate, chopped

1 cup heavy cream

1/3 cup granulated sugar

2 tablespoons chocolate stout

TO MAKE THE BEER ICE CREAM, combine the heavy cream and milk in a medium saucepan over medium heat. Cook, stirring constantly, until the mixture is barely simmering (you will see steam rising from the surface, and small bubbles at the edge of the pan). Remove the pan from the heat and set aside.

In a medium mixing bowl, beat the egg yolks with the sugar and salt until thick and pale yellow. Very slowly whisk 1/4 cup of the hot cream mixture into the egg mixture to temper it. Then transfer the egg mixture to the saucepan with the rest of the cream mixture and return to medium heat. Cook, stirring constantly, for 3 to 6 minutes, or until the mixture has thickened enough to coat the back of a spoon without running.

Remove the saucepan from the heat and strain the mixture through a fine-mesh sieve. Add the vanilla extract and stout. Chill for at least 4 hours or preferably overnight and freeze in an ice cream maker according to the manufacturer's instructions.

TO MAKE THE PROFITEROLES, preheat the oven to 425°F and line a baking sheet with parchment paper.

Combine 1/2 cup water, milk, butter, and salt in a medium saucepan and bring to a boil. Reduce the heat to medium-low, add the flour, and cook, stirring with a wooden spoon, for 1 to 2 minutes, or until the mixture forms a ball and pulls away from the sides of the

(continued on next page)

pan. Transfer the mixture to a mixing bowl and allow it to cool slightly. Using an electric mixer, beat in the eggs, one at a time.

Spoon the mixture into a large, zip-top plastic bag and snip off one of the corners. Squeeze 12 mounds of dough onto the baking sheet, spacing them an inch or two apart. Bake until puffed and golden, about 22 minutes. Turn off the oven, set the door slightly ajar, and allow the profiteroles to rest for another 5 minutes.

Remove the profiteroles from the oven and prick each one with a toothpick to allow steam to escape. Let them cool completely on a wire rack.

TO MAKE THE CHOCOLATE-BEER SAUCE, place the chocolate in a medium bowl. Combine the cream and sugar in a small saucepan and heat over medium-low heat until just barely simmering. Pour the hot cream over the chocolate and stir until the chocolate melts. Stir in the stout.

To assemble the dessert, cut each profiterole in half crosswise. Place a scoop of ice cream on the bottom half of the profiterole and sandwich with the top. Drizzle generously with the chocolate-beer sauce and serve.

SHAKE IT UP: Substitute another richly flavored beer, such as an India Pale Ale, for the stout.

Brown Velvet

4 ounces chilled Champagne or other sparkling wine

4 ounces chocolate stout

Pour the Champagne into a large wine glass.
Very slowly, pour the chocolate stout over the
Champagne so that it floats on top.

**MAKES
1
DRINK**

LUSH AND FRUITY DESSERTS

When I was a kid, every once in a while my mom would serve little bowls of canned fruit cocktail after dinner. I thought it was a total cop-out. I liked the candy red cherries and the pieces of syrupy pineapple, but why were the grapes peeled? And what were those little white chunks? Fruit, I maintained, was not dessert.

Twenty years later I'm still not entirely sure what was in that canned cocktail (Seriously, were those apple pieces? Asian pears?), but I often savor fruit at the end of a meal. I'm not talking about diet-friendly grapefruit halves, though. By "fruit desserts" I mean crisps and crumbles, shortcakes and slumps, most made better with a scoop of ice cream, and all enhanced with alcohol.

Pisco-Roasted Pineapple

PISCO IS A COLORLESS SOUTH AMERICAN LIQUOR. *Similar to wine, it is made from grapes. In the late nineteenth century, a San Francisco bar began serving pisco punch, a potent blend of pisco and pineapple. It has since become the city's signature drink. I've combined those ingredients in a tropical dessert reminiscent of the more traditional rum-roasted pineapple.*

2 tablespoons unsalted butter, melted

¼ cup packed light brown sugar

½ cup pisco

1 medium pineapple, cored and cut crosswise into thick slices

1 or 2 whole nutmeg

Vanilla ice cream, for serving

Preheat the oven to 400°F.

In a medium saucepan, combine the butter, brown sugar, and pisco. Bring to a simmer over medium heat and cook just until the sugar dissolves. Remove the pan from the heat.

Arrange the pineapple slices in single layer in a 13 x 9-inch baking dish. Pour the pisco mixture evenly over the pineapple slices. Add the nutmeg to the dish and roast 20 to 30 minutes, or until the pineapple is tender.

Allow the pineapple slices to cool slightly. To serve, scoop the ice cream into bowls and top with the pineapple slices. Drizzle with the pan juices and serve.

Pisco **Punch**

1 large pineapple, peeled and cut into 1-inch chunks
1 (750 ml) bottle pisco
1¾ cups simple syrup
⅔ cup freshly squeezed lime or lemon juice
Lime or lemon slices, for garnish

Combine the pineapple and pisco in a large jar. Cover and refrigerate
for 2 days, shaking occasionally. Strain the pisco into a large pitcher and
discard the pineapple. Add the simple syrup and the lime or lemon juice.
Stir to blend. Serve in glasses over ice, garnished with a lime or lemon slice.

MAKES ABOUT 12 SERVINGS

Boozy Baked Apples

THE BEST BAKED APPLES TASTE LIKE THE INSIDE OF APPLE PIE: *spicy, warm, and a bit gooey. This version is a true autumn treat, flavored with brown sugar, raisins, maple syrup, and plenty of rum. Watch your apples carefully when they are in the oven. They probably won't be exactly the same size, so some may be done before others.*

My friend Peter makes an insanely delicious version of Hot Buttered Rum. It would be perfect to serve with these apples on a cold winter's night.

6 large baking apples, such as Golden Delicious or Jonagold

⅓ cup packed dark brown sugar

¼ cup raisins

¼ cup chopped pecans or almonds

½ cup plus 3 tablespoons dark rum, divided

3 tablespoons unsalted butter, cut into 6 pieces

½ cup apple cider

3 tablespoons maple syrup

Vanilla ice cream, for serving

Preheat the oven to 375°F. Peel the top third of each apple and scoop out the cores with a melon baller or a paring knife, leaving ½ inch at the bottom.

In a small bowl, combine the sugar, raisins, and the pecans. Place the apples in a 13 x 9-inch baking dish and divide the sugar mixture among the cavities. Drizzle each with ½ tablespoon of rum and top with a piece of butter.

In a medium bowl, whisk the remaining ½ cup rum with the apple cider and the maple syrup. Pour the cider mixture into the dish around the apples. Bake for 30 to 40 minutes, basting with the juices occasionally, or until the apples are just tender but not mushy.

Serve the apples warm, drizzled with the pan juices, and topped with the ice cream.

SHAKE IT UP: Substitute bourbon or scotch for the rum.

Pete's Hot Buttered Rum

¼ pound (1 stick) unsalted butter

½ cup plus 1 tablespoon packed dark brown sugar

1 cup confectioners' sugar

1 cup vanilla ice cream

1 teaspoon ground cinnamon

¼ teaspoon ground ginger

⅛ teaspoon ground nutmeg

2½ cups dark rum, divided

Combine the butter and sugars in a large saucepan over medium heat. Stir constantly until the sugars have dissolved. Remove the saucepan from the heat and stir in the ice cream, cinnamon, ginger, and nutmeg. Transfer the mixture to an airtight plastic container and freeze for at least 4 hours (batter will keep for up to 1 month). Place 1 tablespoon of the ice cream mixture into each of 10 mugs. Add ¼ cup of rum to each mug, and top with hot water.

MAKES
10
SERVINGS

Blackberry Chocolate Romanoff

JEFFREY STEINGARTEN ONCE WROTE A HILARIOUS ARTICLE for Vogue chronicling his plight to make homemade soft-serve ice cream. He tried everything, including purchasing an industrial machine that blew out the power in an entire apartment. I, too, have a bit of an obsession with soft serve. I found that the best way to replicate its airy texture at home was to fold whipped cream into softened ice cream, as in this recipe for classic berry-chocolate romanoff. Now if I could only invent a machine that dispensed soft-serve flavored with booze.

4 cups fresh blackberries, raspberries, or strawberries

¼ cup sugar

¼ cup orange liqueur, such as Grand Marnier

1 pint chocolate ice cream

1 cup heavy whipping cream

2 tablespoons crème de cacao

In a medium bowl, toss the berries, sugar, and the orange liqueur. Place the bowl in the refrigerator and allow to macerate at least 1 hour.

Transfer the ice cream to the refrigerator to soften while preparing the whipped cream. In a large bowl using an electric mixer, whip the cream with the crème de cacao until soft peaks form. Fold in the softened ice cream.

Divide the cream mixture between 6 bowls. Top with the berries and serve.

Tropical Fruit Foster

BANANAS FOSTER HAILS FROM NEW ORLEANS, *a city that is also famous for its cocktails, so it should come as no surprise that the fiery, fruity dessert is saturated with booze. I've given the traditional version a twist with fresh mango and coconut rum. Since you must be extremely cautious when igniting the fruit mixture, don't indulge in a Tropical Hurricane until after you've finished making the dessert!*

4 tablespoons (½ stick)
    unsalted butter

1 cup lightly packed dark
    brown sugar

¼ teaspoon ground
    cinnamon

¼ cup coconut rum

3 slightly under-ripe
    bananas, peeled, cut in
    half lengthwise and then
    crosswise

1 ripe mango, peeled, cored,
    and cut into ½-inch wedges

⅓ cup dark rum

Vanilla ice cream,
    for serving

In a large heavy-bottomed skillet, melt the butter with the brown sugar and cinnamon over medium-low heat. Cook until the sugar dissolves. Add the coconut rum and stir to combine.

Arrange the banana and mango wedges in the pan so they are spaced evenly and not overlapping too much. Cook for 1 to 2 minutes, and then flip the fruit and cook for 1 to 2 minutes more on the other side. Using a slotted spoon, transfer the banana and mango pieces to a serving bowl.

Carefully pour the dark rum into the pan with the remaining sugar mixture and continue to cook for 1 or 2 minutes, or until the mixture is heated. Very carefully, ignite the mixture with a long match. Cook for 1 or 2 minutes, or until the flames die out and the mixture is syrupy.

Divide the banana and mango pieces between individual serving bowls. Top with the sauce and scoops of vanilla ice cream, and serve.

Tropical Hurricanes

1½ cups pineapple juice

1½ cups mango nectar
or mango juice

¼ cup freshly squeezed lemon juice

4 ounces coconut rum

4 ounces dark rum

4 ounces grenadine

4 slices of orange

4 fresh cherries

In a large pitcher, combine the pineapple juice, mango nectar, lemon juice, coconut rum, dark rum, and grenadine. Stir well. Fill 4 glasses with ice and divide the mixture between them. Garnish each drink with a slice of orange and a cherry.

MAKES
4
DRINKS

Saucy Prunes with Cinnamon and Honey

MAKES ABOUT 2½ CUPS OR 8 SERVINGS

SOMEWHERE ALONG THE LINE, *prunes got lumped into the category of "old people food," along with tomato juice and soft-boiled eggs. But prunes are actually quite chic (well, as chic as dried fruit can be). Plump, moist, and sweet, they are a natural match for spicy cinnamon and rich red wine. These prunes will last for up to a month in the refrigerator. I think they taste best over chocolate ice cream, but for a quick weeknight dessert, use whatever flavor is in your freezer.*

1 (12-ounce) package pitted prunes

2 cinnamon sticks

¼ teaspoon ground nutmeg

1 tablespoon sugar

2 tablespoons honey

¼ cup water

1 cup dry red wine

2 pints chocolate ice cream, for serving

Combine the prunes, cinnamon sticks, nutmeg, sugar, honey, wine, and ¼ cup water in a medium saucepot. Bring to a boil over medium heat, and then reduce the heat and simmer until the prunes are very tender, about 20 minutes.

With a slotted spoon, transfer the prunes to a medium bowl. Set aside. Return the wine mixture to a boil and cook until reduced and syrupy, about 5 minutes. Remove the cinnamon sticks from the pot and discard.

Pour the wine over the prunes and allow the mixture to cool, uncovered, to room temperature. Cover and refrigerate until cold. To serve, spoon the sauce over scoops of chocolate ice cream.

Pear and Red Grape
Turnovers

IN MANY HIGH-END LIQUOR STORES, *you will see bottles of pear brandy with a whole pear inside. They always remind me of the model ships-in-a-bottle one of my friend's grandfathers used to make. How did they get in there? I'm not sure about the boats, but to make the brandy, distillers tie empty bottles onto the developing branches of pear trees so that the fruits grow inside. These turnovers make an excellent lazy weekend breakfast.*

2 small pears, peeled, cored, and cut into ½-inch chunks (about 1½ cups)

1 cup seedless red grapes, halved

¼ cup sugar

1 tablespoon cornstarch

¼ teaspoon ground cinnamon

3 tablespoons pear brandy or brandy

1 sheet (half a 17.2-ounce package) frozen puff pastry, defrosted

1 large egg, lightly beaten with 2 teaspoons water

Line a baking sheet with parchment paper.

In a medium bowl, combine the pears, grapes, sugar, cornstarch, cinnamon, and brandy. Toss gently to evenly coat the fruit.

On a lightly floured work surface, roll the puff pastry sheet out into a 12 x 12-inch square. Using a sharp knife, cut the pastry into 6 equal squares.

Place a scoop of the pear mixture into the center of a square. Brush the edges with the egg wash and fold the pastry diagonally over the filling. Crimp the edges with a fork to seal. Brush the top of the pastry with more of the egg wash and cut 2 or 3 small vents in the top. Transfer the pastry to the baking sheet. Repeat with remaining pastry squares and pear mixture. Transfer the baking sheet to the refrigerator and chill for 20 minutes.

Preheat the oven to 400°F. Bake the turnovers for 20 to 23 minutes, or until they are puffed and golden. Serve warm or at room temperature.

SHAKE IT UP: Substitute bourbon, dark rum, or orange liqueur for the brandy.

Nectarine-Raspberry Dutch Baby

MAKES 6 SERVINGS

A DUTCH BABY IS LIKE A LARGE, RUSTIC PANCAKE. *It is cut into wedges and served warm, straight from the skillet, showered in confectioners' sugar. I started making Dutch babies around the time my mom passed on my grandmother's cast iron skillet to me (talk about well-seasoned!). This summery version is one of my favorites.*

3 large eggs

1 teaspoon freshly grated lemon zest

⅓ cup granulated sugar

¼ teaspoon salt

⅔ cup all-purpose flour

¼ teaspoon ground cinnamon

⅓ cup plus 2 tablespoons milk

3 tablespoons white wine

1 cup raspberries

2 medium nectarines, cut into 1-inch chunks

4 tablespoons (½ stick) unsalted butter

Confectioners' sugar, for dusting

Preheat the oven to 425°F. On the stovetop, heat a 10-inch cast iron skillet over medium heat.

In a medium bowl, beat the eggs, lemon zest, sugar, and salt with an electric mixer until combined. Add the flour, cinnamon, milk, and wine and beat until smooth. Stir in the raspberries and the nectarines.

Melt the butter in the skillet and swirl the pan to coat it. Pour the batter into the skillet, making sure to spread the fruit evenly. Transfer the skillet, to the oven and bake for 20 to 25 minutes, or until puffed and golden brown.

Dust with confectioners' sugar and serve hot.

SHAKE IT UP: Substitute Calvados (apple-flavored brandy) for the wine and apples for the nectarines.

White Wine Sangria

1 (750 ml) bottle dry white wine, such as sauvignon blanc

½ cup orange liqueur, such as Grand Marnier

½ cup peach brandy or peach schnapps

½ cup tropical fruit juice,
such as Tropicana Orange Peach Mango

1 large peach, cut into ½-inch chunks

1 small orange, cut into thin wheels

1 lime, cut into thin wheels

In a large pitcher, combine the wine, orange liqueur,
peach brandy, and fruit juice. Stir to blend. Add the peach, orange slices,
and lime slices. Refrigerate until well chilled, about 2 hours.
Serve in wine glasses over ice.

MAKES
6
SERVINGS

Drunken Pear Crisps

I LOVE POACHED PEARS, BUT WHENEVER *I have them for dessert I'm left wanting a little something more, like a crunchy cookie or a giant scoop of vanilla ice cream. This dessert is a lot like a traditional apple crisp, except that the apples have been replaced by wine-saturated pears. For this recipe I use a cheap-but-decent merlot, and drink the last glass while the crisps are in the oven.*

FOR THE PEARS:

2 cups water

2 cups dry red wine, preferably merlot

1 cup orange juice

1 cup granulated sugar

4 strips orange zest

1 cinnamon stick

4 whole cloves

6 firm-ripe pears, peeled, halved, and cored

FOR THE CRISP TOPPING:

1½ cups all-purpose flour

1¼ cups old-fashioned rolled oats

½ cup granulated sugar

½ cup packed dark brown sugar

Pinch of salt

½ cup (1 stick) unsalted butter, diced

Vanilla ice cream, for serving

FOR THE PEARS, combine the 2 cups of water, the wine, orange juice, sugar, orange zest, cinnamon stick, and cloves in a pot large enough to hold all the pear halves in a single layer. Bring to a boil over medium heat, stirring until sugar dissolves. Remove from heat. Add the pears, round side down, and return the liquid to a simmer over medium heat. Simmer, basting the pears occasionally, about 30 minutes. Remove the pears from the cooking liquid with a slotted spoon and set aside in a medium bowl.

Strain the liquid, discarding the solids. Return the liquid to a heat and boil until it is reduced slightly, about 15 minutes. Pour the syrup over the pears and refrigerate until pears are cool, about 2 hours.

Preheat the oven to 350°F.

Remove the pears from the refrigerator and cut them into ½-inch dice. Divide them between six 5-ounce ramekins or custard cups. Drizzle each with about 2 tablespoons of the cooking liquid. Set aside. Discard the remaining cooking liquid or reserve for another use.

TO MAKE THE CRISP TOPPING, combine the flour, oats, sugar, brown sugar, and salt in a medium bowl. Using a pastry blender, two knives, or clean fingers, work the butter into the flour mixture until it forms coarse crumbs. Sprinkle the topping evenly over the pears.

Place the ramekins on a baking sheet and bake until the filling bubbles and the topping is golden, about 30 minutes. Cool 10 minutes. Serve warm with scoops of vanilla ice cream on top.

Bourbon Apple Crisp

SINCE I'M A FOOD WRITER AND A BAKER, *people usually expect my favorite dessert to be some wildly fancy and sophisticated concoction. But really what I love best is simple, no-frills apple crisp, served warm with a big scoop of vanilla ice cream. For the holidays, I often reduce the apples to 6 cups and add 2 cups of fresh cranberries. If you don't have maple syrup, substitute granulated sugar.*

FOR THE TOPPING:

1 cup all-purpose flour

½ cup packed light brown sugar

½ teaspoon ground cinnamon

¼ teaspoon salt

¼ pound (1 stick) unsalted butter, cut into ½-inch chunks

½ cup old-fashioned rolled oats (not instant)

FOR THE FILLING:

3 pounds tart baking apples, peeled and sliced ⅓-inch thick (about 8 cups)

3 tablespoons maple syrup

3 tablespoons bourbon

1 tablespoon lemon juice

Preheat the oven to 375°F.

TO MAKE THE TOPPING, combine the flour, brown sugar, cinnamon, and salt in the work bowl of a food processor and pulse to blend. Add the butter, a few pieces at a time, and pulse until the mixture resembles coarse meal. Pour the mixture into a medium bowl and stir in the oats.

TO MAKE THE FILLING, place the apples in a large bowl and add the maple syrup, bourbon, and lemon juice. Toss well to coat. Pour the apple mixture into a 9-inch square baking dish. Sprinkle the topping evenly over the apples and bake for about 35 minutes, or until the topping is golden and the apples are bubbling. Cool the crisp on a wire rack and serve warm or at room temperature.

SHAKE IT UP: Substitute dark rum or brandy for the bourbon.

Maple Leaf

2 ounces bourbon
½ ounce pure maple syrup
½ ounce lemon juice
1 cinnamon stick

Combine the bourbon, maple syrup, and lemon juice
in a cocktail shaker filled with ice. Shake and strain
into a cocktail glass. Garnish with the cinnamon stick.

MAKES
1
DRINK

Rhubarb-Rosé Crisp

WHITE ZINFANDEL IS OFTEN THE BUTT OF WINE JOKES. *It's true that the sweet, pink wine isn't exactly the most sophisticated varietal, but it works wonders in this fruity rhubarb crisp topped with cinnamon-spiced oats. It's especially delicious served with vanilla ice cream or peach sherbet.*

**FOR THE
RHUBARB FILLING:**

2 to 2½ pounds rhubarb,
    cut into 1-inch chunks
    (about 6 cups)

Zest of 1 large lemon

1 cup granulated sugar

1 cup plus 2 tablespoons
    rosé wine, divided

1 (2-inch) cinnamon stick

Half of a vanilla bean, split
    lengthwise

2 tablespoons cornstarch

FOR THE TOPPING:

⅔ cup old-fashioned
    rolled oats

½ cup all-purpose flour

½ cup packed light
    brown sugar

½ teaspoon ground
    cinnamon

¼ teaspoon salt

6 tablespoons (¾ stick)
    unsalted butter, softened

Preheat the oven to 375°F.

TO MAKE THE RHUBARB FILLING, combine the rhubarb and lemon zest in a 9 x 9-inch baking pan and set aside.

Combine the sugar, 1 cup of the wine, cinnamon stick, and vanilla bean in a medium saucepan. Bring to a simmer over medium heat and simmer, stirring occasionally, until the sugar dissolves. Meanwhile, combine the remaining 2 tablespoons of the wine with the cornstarch in a small bowl and stir until well blended.

When the sugar has dissolved, add the cornstarch mixture to the saucepan and simmer until the filling thickens and turns clear, 1 to 3 minutes. It should be the consistency of runny pudding. Remove the saucepan from the heat and allow to cool while you make the topping.

TO MAKE THE TOPPING, combine the rolled oats, flour, light brown sugar, cinnamon, and salt in a medium bowl. Add the butter and, using a fork or clean fingers, work it into the oat mixture until it is evenly distributed and the mixture is crumbly and a bit clumpy.

Remove the cinnamon stick and vanilla bean from the wine mixture, and then pour the wine mixture over the rhubarb. Stir gently to make sure all the pieces of rhubarb are evenly coated. Sprinkle the topping evenly over the filling and bake for 30 to 40 minutes, or until the topping is golden brown and the filling is bubbling.

Winter Berry Gratin

BERRY GRATINS ARE TYPICALLY MADE WITH MARSALA, *an Italian fortified wine similar to port. I've substituted ice wine, which is made from frozen grapes. Ice wine has a zingy, sweet flavor and is a refreshing alternative to heavier after-dinner liqueurs. German ice wines* (eiswein) *can be quite expensive. Look for more affordable Canadian versions.*

2 cups fresh cranberries

2 cups fresh or frozen raspberries

½ cup granulated sugar, divided

¼ cup plus 2 tablespoons ice wine

4 large egg yolks

2 tablespoons mascarpone or sour cream

Preheat the oven to 400°F and position a rack in the upper third. Combine the cranberries, raspberries, ¼ cup of the sugar, and 2 tablespoons of the ice wine in a gratin dish and toss to coat.

Combine the remaining ¼ cup sugar, the remaining ¼ cup ice wine, and the egg yolks in a large glass bowl. Place the bowl over a saucepan of simmering water. Beat the mixture with an electric mixer until it is frothy and thick, about 4 minutes. Remove the bowl from the heat and allow the mixture to cool slightly, for about 5 minutes.

Gently fold the mascarpone or sour cream into the yolk mixture. Pour over the berries and bake until the topping is bubbly and glazed, about 1 to 2 minutes. Serve immediately.

SHAKE IT UP: Substitute marsala or Sauternes for the ice wine.

Blueberry-Port Slump with Almond Dumplings

MAKES 6 SERVINGS

A SLUMP (SOMETIMES CALLED A GRUNT, *but I think that's less appetizing) is a homey, fruit-based dessert that is "baked" in a covered skillet on the stovetop. Sometimes as it cooks, moisture escapes from the skillet and makes a "grunting" sound. Once served, it "slumps" messily into bowls rather than holding its shape. The richness of the port in this recipe really brings out the blueberry flavor. While it's best with fresh summer berries, you can use frozen blueberries in a pinch. Serve with ice cream or whipped cream.*

FOR THE BLUEBERRIES:

4 cups blueberries

½ cup sugar

¼ cup ruby port

½ cup water

2 tablespoons fresh lemon juice

¼ teaspoon ground cinnamon

¼ teaspoon ground nutmeg

FOR THE ALMOND DUMPLINGS:

¾ cup all-purpose flour

½ cup slivered almonds, toasted

3 tablespoons sugar

1 teaspoon baking powder

¼ teaspoon salt

3 tablespoons unsalted butter, chilled and diced

¼ cup buttermilk or milk

TO MAKE THE BLUEBERRY FILLING, combine the blueberries, sugar, port, ½ cup water, lemon juice, cinnamon, and nutmeg in a 12-inch skillet. Bring to a boil over medium heat, and then reduce the heat and simmer until berries soften just a bit, 4 to 5 minutes.

TO MAKE THE DUMPLINGS, combine the flour, almonds, sugar, baking powder, and salt in the work bowl of a food processor and pulse to blend. Add the butter, a few chunks at a time, and pulse to blend. Add the buttermilk and pulse until the mixture comes together in a ball.

Drop heaping tablespoons of the dough over the blueberry mixture. Reduce the heat to low, cover the skillet, and simmer until the dumplings are firm to the touch and a toothpick inserted into the center of one comes out clean, 20 to 25 minutes. Scoop the slump into bowls and serve warm.

SHAKE IT UP: Substitute red wine for the port.

Gingery Peach Cobbler

MAKES 6 SERVINGS

I LOVE THE FRESH, SPICY FLAVOR OF GINGER, *but I'm not a huge fan of the sugary crystallized stuff. Ginger liqueur is a great way to add subtle, even flavor without too much bite. In this recipe it adds a refreshing twist to a classic "back porch" summer dessert. Depending on the juiciness of your peaches, you may need slightly more or less cornstarch. Serve topped with ginger ice cream, if you can find it, or vanilla.*

FOR THE FRUIT:

3 pounds peaches, halved, pitted, and cut into ½-inch slices

3 tablespoons cornstarch

2 tablespoons sugar

¼ cup ginger liqueur, such as Domaine de Canton

FOR THE TOPPING:

1½ cups all-purpose flour

¼ cup plus 1 tablespoon sugar, divided

2 teaspoons baking powder

½ teaspoon salt

¼ teaspoon ground ginger

6 tablespoons cold unsalted butter, diced

½ cup heavy cream or whole milk

2 tablespoons ginger liqueur, such as Domaine de Canton

Preheat the oven to 375°F.

TO MAKE THE FRUIT, toss the peaches with the cornstarch, sugar, and ginger liqueur in a large bowl. Pour the fruit mixture into a 9-inch square baking dish and bake just until the fruit begins to bubble, 8 to 10 minutes.

TO MAKE THE TOPPING, combine the flour, ½ cup of the sugar, the baking powder, and salt in the work bowl of a food processor and pulse to combine. Add the butter and pulse until the mixture resembles coarse meal. Add the cream and the ginger liqueur and pulse just until a dough forms.

Drop the dough in 6 mounds on top of the fruit mixture. Sprinkle the mounds with the remaining 1 tablespoon sugar and return the cobbler to the oven. Bake for 20 to 25 minutes, or until the topping is golden brown and the fruit is bubbling. Cool the cobbler on a wire rack for at least 30 minutes.

SHAKE IT UP: Substitute almond liqueur or bourbon for the ginger liqueur, and omit the ground ginger.

Ginger **Highball**

1½ ounces bourbon
1 ounce ginger liqueur, such as Domaine de Canton
¾ ounce freshly squeezed lemon juice
1 teaspoon superfine sugar
2 ounces club soda

Combine the bourbon, ginger liqueur, lemon juice,
and sugar in a cocktail shaker filled with ice. Shake and strain into a
highball glass filled with ice. Top with the club soda.

MAKES
1
DRINK

Strawberry and Honey Shortcake

I THINK OF THIS AS MY "WINNIE THE POOH DESSERT." *There is something delightfully childish about strawberry shortcake, and this version is infused with over-the-top honey flavor. Of course, it's best with local, peak-of-the-season fruit, so save this recipe for the summer.*

FOR THE STRAWBERRY FILLING:

4 cups ripe strawberries, stemmed and sliced

2 tablespoons granulated sugar

2 tablespoons honey liqueur, such as Bärenjäger, Krupnik, or Wild Turkey American Honey

FOR THE SHORTCAKE:

2 cups all-purpose flour

¼ cup granulated sugar

1 tablespoon baking powder

¼ teaspoon salt

¼ pound (1 stick) unsalted butter, cut into ½-inch pieces

½ cup heavy cream

¼ cup honey liqueur

FOR THE WHIPPED CREAM:

1¼ cups heavy cream

2 tablespoons confectioners' sugar

1 tablespoon honey liqueur

Preheat the oven to 450°F. Grease an 8 x 8-inch square pan with butter, or spray it with nonstick spray.

TO MAKE THE STRAWBERRY FILLING, combine the strawberries with the sugar and the honey liqueur in a medium bowl. Mash them lightly and stir them around a bit with a fork. Cover the bowl with plastic wrap and chill.

TO MAKE THE SHORTCAKES, combine the flour, sugar, baking powder, and salt in the work bowl of a food processor and pulse to combine. Add the butter, a few chunks at a time, and pulse until incorporated. Add the cream and the honey liqueur and pulse until a lumpy batter forms.

Spread the batter into the prepared pan, smoothing it as evenly as you can. (It will look a bit sloppy, but that's all part of a shortcake's charm.) Bake the shortcake for 10 to 15 minutes, or until a toothpick inserted into the center comes out clean. Allow the shortcake to cool in the pan.

TO MAKE THE WHIPPED CREAM, beat the cream with the confectioners' sugar and the honey liqueur in a large bowl until soft peaks form.

Cut the shortcake into six squares and slice each square in half horizontally. Scoop large spoonfuls of the mashed strawberries over the bottom half of each piece of shortcake and cover with the top pieces of cake. Scoop spoonfuls of berries over the tops, and then dollop with whipped cream. Serve immediately.

SHAKE IT UP: Substitute almond liqueur, such as amaretto, for the honey liqueur.

Chocolate Pavlova with Cranberry-Orange Sauce

A PAVLOVA IS AN AIRY ALTERNATIVE TO A HEAVIER LAYER CAKE, *yet it looks just as festive. This dessert has multiple steps, but don't let that deter you. The cranberry-orange sauce can be made up to two days ahead, and the meringue can be baked a day in advance and stored loosely wrapped at room temperature. For a perfectly crisp meringue, make sure to prepare it on a sunny day. If there is moisture in the air, it will come out chewy.*

FOR THE MERINGUE:

5 large egg whites, at room temperature

¼ teaspoon cream of tartar

1 cup superfine sugar

1 teaspoon orange liqueur, such as Grand Marnier or Triple Sec

3 tablespoons Dutch-process cocoa powder

FOR THE CRANBERRY-ORANGE SAUCE:

1 cup fresh cranberries

½ cup granulated sugar

¾ cup orange marmalade

2 tablespoons orange liqueur, such as Grand Marnier or Triple Sec

FOR THE WHIPPED CREAM:

1 cup heavy cream

2 tablespoons granulated sugar

1 tablespoon plus 1 teaspoon orange liqueur, such as Grand Marnier or Triple Sec

Preheat the oven to 275°F. Line a baking sheet with parchment paper and draw an 8-inch circle in the middle.

TO MAKE THE MERINGUE, beat the egg whites with an electric mixer in a large bowl until foamy. Add the cream of tartar and beat until soft peaks form. With the electric mixer running, add the sugar, 1 tablespoon at a time, and beat until stiff peaks form. Carefully fold the orange liqueur into the egg whites with a spatula. Sift the cocoa over the egg whites and fold in carefully.

Gently spread the meringue onto the circle on the parchment paper and bake until the meringue is dry to the touch, about 1 hour and 15 minutes. Turn off the oven, prop open the door, and allow the meringue to cool completely in the oven.

TO MAKE THE CRANBERRY-ORANGE SAUCE, combine the cranberries, sugar, and ¼ cup water in a small saucepan. Bring to a boil over medium heat and cook until the cranberries soften and just begin to burst, about 5 minutes. Whisk in the marmalade and the orange liqueur until smooth. Transfer to a bowl, cover, and chill.

TO MAKE THE WHIPPED CREAM, beat the heavy cream, sugar, and orange liqueur with an electric mixer in a large bowl until soft peaks form, about 3 minutes.

To assemble the Pavlova, place the meringue on a large serving plate. Spread the whipped cream evenly over the meringue, and spoon the cranberry mixture into the middle. Serve immediately.

ABOUT THE AUTHOR

ots of people say that, given her name, Lucy Baker was destined for a culinary career. In fact, many of her earliest memories revolve around food, from helping her mother bake saucepan brownies on Saturday afternoons to grocery shopping with her father and snacking on Pepperidge Farm cookies straight from the bag.

Lucy is currently a food writer and recipe tester, and a contributing columnist for SeriousEats.com. She has written articles for numerous publications, both online and in print, including *Edible Brooklyn, Publishers Weekly, Popular Mechanics,* and *Time Out New York.* She was the recipe tester for *The Veselka Cookbook,* and a co-writer for *The Fat Witch Brownie Book.* For three years, she worked as an assistant cookbook editor at HarperCollins Publishers, and she holds an MFA in creative writing. She lives in Brooklyn, New York.

FORMULAS FOR METRIC CONVERSION

FORMULAS FOR METRIC CONVERSION

Ounces to grams	multiply ounces by 28.35
Pounds to grams	multiply pounds by 453.5
Cups to liters	multiply cups by .24
Fahrenheit to Centigrade	subtract 32 from Fahrenheit, multiply by 5 and divide by 9

METRIC EQUIVALENTS FOR VOLUME

U.S.		Metric
$1/8$ tsp.		0.6 ml
$1/2$ tsp.		2.5 ml
$3/4$ tsp.		4.0 ml
1 tsp.		5.0 ml
$1^1/2$ tsp.		7.0 ml
2 tsp.		10.0 ml
3 tsp.		15.0 ml
4 tsp.		20.0 ml
1 Tbsp.	—	15.0 ml
$1^1/2$ Tbsp.	—	22.0 ml
2 Tbsp. ($1/8$ cup)	1 fl. oz	30.0 ml
$2^1/2$ Tbsp.	—	37.0 ml
3 Tbsp.	—	44.0 ml
$1/3$ cup	—	57.0 ml
4 Tbsp. ($1/4$ cup)	2 fl. oz	59.0 ml
5 Tbsp.	—	74.0 ml
6 Tbsp.	—	89.0 ml
8 Tbsp. ($1/2$ cup)	4 fl. oz	120.0 ml
$3/4$ cup	6 fl. oz	178.0 ml
1 cup	8 fl. oz	237.0 ml (.24 liters)
$1^1/2$ cups	—	354.0 ml
$1^3/4$ cups	—	414.0 ml
2 cups (1 pint)	16 fl. oz	473.0 ml
4 cups (1 quart)	32 fl. oz	(.95 liters)
5 cups	—	(1.183 liters)
16 cups (1 gallon)	128 fl. oz	(3.8 liters)

OVEN TEMPERATURES

Degrees Fahrenheit	Degrees Centigrade	British Gas Marks
200°	93°	—
250°	120°	—
275°	140°	1
300°	150°	2
325°	165°	3
350°	175°	4
375°	190°	5
400°	200°	6
450°	230°	8

METRIC EQUIVALENTS FOR BUTTER

U.S.	Metric
2 tsp.	10.0 g
1 Tbsp.	15.0 g
1¹/₂ Tbsp.	22.5 g
2 Tbsp. (1 oz)	55.0 g
3 Tbsp.	70.0 g
¹/₄ lb. (1 stick)	110.0 g
¹/₂ lb. (2 sticks)	220.0 g

METRIC EQUIVALENTS FOR LENGTH

U.S.	Metric
¹/₄ inch	.65 cm
¹/₂ inch	1.25 cm
1 inch	2.50 cm
2 inches	5.00 cm
3 inches	6.00 cm
4 inches	8.00 cm
5 inches	11.00 cm
6 inches	15.00 cm
7 inches	18.00 cm
8 inches	20.00 cm
9 inches	23.00 cm
12 inches	30.50 cm
15 inches	38.00 cm

METRIC EQUIVALENTS FOR WEIGHT

U.S.	Metric
1 oz	28 g
2 oz	58 g
3 oz	85 g
4 oz (¹/₄ lb.)	113 g
5 oz	142 g
6 oz	170 g
7 oz	199 g
8 oz (¹/₂ lb.)	227 g
10 oz	284 g
12 oz (³/₄ lb.)	340 g
14 oz	397 g
16 oz (1 lb.)	454 g

Source: Herbst, Sharon Tyler. *The Food Lover's Companion*. 3rd ed. Hauppauge: Barron's, 2001.

INDEX

R

S

T